The Invisible Grief of Adulthood

Letters from the Sun for What You Can't Say Out Loud

\+

The Return System for What Hurts

STANDARD EDITION

By The Sun

Transcribed by Dr. Nikkia R. Gumbs, Ed.D.

Standard Edition
Published by The House of the Sun, LLC
www.thehouseofthesun.com
www.invisible-grief.com

Front and back cover designs and artwork by Nikkia Gumbs

The House of the Sun™ Presents: The Invisible Grief Series™ trademark pending

ISBN: 979-8-9994881-1-4

Library of Congress Control Number: 2025917602

Printed in the United States of America

To my mom, Gloria, who always said I would write a book.
I don't think anyone else could have been mother to the Sun.

And for everyone still aching for what they were told not to grieve.

TABLE OF CONTENTS

LETTERS FROM THE SUN

A Letter From The Sun

This book will not save you.

It isn't a plan.
It won't tell you who to become.
But it **will** tell the truth.

These letters are soul portraits
not of who you perform as,
but who you are
when no one's watching.

The parts you hide.
The ache you explain away.
The ordinary emptiness
no one warns you about.

They aren't here to fix you.
They're here to name what hurts
before you vanish inside it.

What you're holding is a
form of **soul witnessing**
the sacred act of seeing someone
without trying
to change them,
fix them.

These letters do that in written form.
They meet what has been
unnamed,
unseen,
unclaimed
and say: *I see it. I won't look away.*

Some will hit like a punch.

Others, like a balm.

Some won't be for you at all.

But the one that is?
You'll know.
You'll feel it in your chest.
Behind your eyes.
In the silence after.

You'll say: **"That's it.
That's the thing I never
knew how to say."**

—The Sun

A Few Notes Before You Begin

What is Spell-Lit™?

Spell-Lit™ is a literary genre that blends emotional rupture, poetic structure, and breath-work formatting. The term stands for *Spellwork Literature*…writing that doesn't just describe a feeling, but enacts it on the page. It draws from grief texts, line-broken memoir, ritual performance, and somatic poetics to create an embodied reading experience.

Each letter in this book is written in the Spell-Lit™ style: short stanzas, frequent line breaks, and precise spacing meant to mirror the rhythm of emotion in the body and pace the reader. These aren't poems or essays. They're spells of remembrance for griefs that usually go unnamed.

In its full form, Spell-Lit™ uses custom-designed glyphs that act as visual cues for somatic movement: clapping, pausing, turning the head, exhaling, etc. These glyphs signal when to move the body, when to breathe, and when to sit with a rupture. But this edition, what you're holding, is the **standard edition**, which does **not** include glyphs. Due to current limitations in publishing technology (and the fact that I built this alone, with no design team), this edition contains only the text and line breaks of each letter. A full Spell-Lit™ edition will be released in the future with all glyphs and somatic cues included.

The current Spell-Lit™ formatting protocol (at the time of publishing) is defined in the **Spell-Lit™ Codex v2.0**, which was finalized *after* the completion of this manuscript. As a result, not every letter in this book adheres perfectly to v2.0 standards. Still, the spirit, structure, and cadence remain true to the genre. When future editions are released, they may include updated formatting aligned with the latest version of the Codex.

A formal white paper and academic article are also underway to codify Spell-Lit™ as a legitimate literary form and support its adoption in university classrooms, trauma literacy courses, and grief education settings. The goal is to protect the emotional and somatic integrity of this work as it moves beyond a single book.

How to Use This Book

This is not just a book.

It's an instrument with two parts:

Letters from the Sun and a Return System™

Each letter is a shard. A key. A mirror.

Some will cut. Some will unlock. Some will echo grief you haven't named in years.

Do not binge this. This is not a book you read all at once.
The weight will stay with you.

Here's how to engage without losing yourself:

- **Skim the titles.** Let your body choose. Curiosity is enough.

- **Read them slowly.** The line breaks are there for a reason. And do not read more than 5 in a single sitting.

- **Breathe like it matters.** This isn't metaphor. If a line knocks the wind out of you, stay there. If a phrase makes your chest tighten, don't skip ahead. Grief will try to make you scroll past the moment. Don't let it. Treat each section like a breathwork sequence:
  > One blank line = one breath.
  > Two blank lines = full exhale and reset.
  If you need to close the book, do. If you need to scream, do. If you need to write in the margins, please do. This is a nervous system-compatible text.

- **Don't stop halfway though a letter.** You might catch the blade and miss the balm.

- **Take notes.** What stirs you will change. You'll come back differently.

- **When it hits…pause.** Walk. Cry. Text someone. Put the book down.

  - **When it hits hard, use Return System tools.** At the end of this book, you'll find a Return System: short, body-based rituals for nervous system repair. If a letter cracks something open, don't white-knuckle your way through it. Go to page 397 and make your way back to yourself.

- ○ **If your system begins to crash, go directly to the Break Glass protocols on page 438.** Pick the one that matches how you are feeling.

Content Note

This book names griefs that often go unspoken: trauma, loss, estrangement, rage, despair. Some letters may surface difficult emotions or memories. That is intentional. For when the ache rises, the Return System beginning on page 397 offers somatic tools to help you stay with yourself.

What Is The Return System™?

This book doesn't just name the grief. It shows you how to survive it.

You're not holding a poetry book. You're holding a living system. A body of letters *and* a body of rituals (somatic exercises). Built together to be used together.

Some of what you read in these pages may rupture something in you. Not because it's cruel. Because it's *true*. And when truth makes contact, it moves. It stirs. It burns. It floods the system.

That's not the end of the book.

That's the middle.

After the 111 letters, you'll find **The Return System™**: a four-part, body-based framework for staying with yourself when the ache rises.

Not concepts. Not affirmations. **Real practices.** For when you want to throw the book across the room and still need a way back into your own body.

The Return System™ Includes

- **Return Rites** - for when your system is shaky but intact
- **Restoration Rites** - for when emotion floods the body
- **Break Glass Protocols** - for acute moments of panic, collapse, or rage
- **Emergency Intervention Kit** - with support tools for all identities, needs, and abilities

This book doesn't assume you're okay. It builds you a way back for when you're not.

You can skip the letters and go straight to the exercises. You can cry your way through and return at the end. You can stop halfway, tear a page out, and use that as your lifeline.

There is no right way. Only the **way you find yourself again.**

This is that way.

You Are Invited To Write Your Own Letter.
At the end of this book, there's space to write your own letter. If you are unsure where to start, go back to the letters in this book that made you feel something. There is nothing wrong with stitching together lines and phrases from a variety of letters to craft your own. Writing it makes you more than a reader. It makes you a participant. A witness. *A spell-breaker.*

Once complete, you can keep it. You can read it aloud or burn it (safely). Or you can submit it anonymously and add your voice to the collective altar of invisible grief at www.invisible-grief.com.

What This Book Isn't
This isn't a memoir. This isn't a fix. This isn't a journey with a clean arc. It's a mirror. A cracked, honest, sometimes unbearable mirror. The hope isn't that you'll fix what you find here, but that you'll finally name it.

Why Are Some Letters Gendered?
These letters are universal. In this volume, two letter titles are gendered and others use specific pronouns to shape the emotional tone, but that doesn't mean they're off-limits to anyone. You might not be a woman disappearing in her marriage (Letter 39). But you may resonate with the feeling of losing yourself inside of a relationship. What matters most is the feeling. And *that* is universal.

Why Do Some Letters Sound Similar?
Some letters overlap in theme and language, but the entry point is microscopically different. Feelings are tricky like that. Two people can live through the same thing and carry it in slightly or very different ways.

This isn't repetition. It's refinement. It's the way grief circles back with a slightly different face.

What Is In This Book?
This book includes:
- 111 Letters from the Sun
- Full Return System
- Journal pages to capture letters that resonate
- Journal pages to write your own letter

Why Are The Letters Numbered?
To make them easier to find, reference, and return to.

Is This Connected To Religion Or Spiritual Group?
No. This book is not affiliated with any institution. Words like *holy* and *sacred* appear throughout, but they're used in the spirit of meaning, not doctrine. This is a book for the soul, not a system.

What Is With All The White Space?
Because grief needs room. Because your nervous system is already overstimulated. Because your body reads *layout* before it reads *words*. Because this isn't a beach read…it's a mirror. And you can't meet your truth if it's crammed between margins like an afterthought.

This isn't just style. It's function. Each pause, each line break, each breath is intentional. White space is part of the spell.

It's how we slow you down enough to feel what you usually skip.

This is also a workbook. Highlight it. Underline the lines that land like lightning. Write in the margins. Circle phrases. Draw. Spill tears on the page.

This isn't a book to keep pristine. It's a *field manual*…meant to be carried, cracked open, lived with. Used right, it becomes a personal record: part witness, part journal, part survival map.

By the end, it should look like it's *been through something with you*. Because it has.

Accessibility Note
This book was written for every body.

Grief lives in all bodies. But not all bodies move, speak, feel, or perceive in the same ways.

Every exercise in this book was crafted with that truth in mind. Many include **alternate versions** for people navigating chronic pain, illness, fatigue, paralysis, neurodivergence, sensory sensitivity, trauma, or mobility differences. Others contain embedded notes offering **symbolic**, **silent**, or **imagined** adaptations. No version is lesser. All are valid.

Wherever possible, exercises are designed to be done:

- **Lying down or seated**
- **Without speaking aloud**
- **Without standing, walking, or using full body motion**
- **With limited or no sensation**
- **With minimal resources, in institutional settings, or alone**

You do not need to perform the ritual "perfectly" to receive its medicine.
You do not need to speak, move, or feel in order to belong.

A Note On Print Format

This book was designed in print format first, with great care given to **structure, line breaks, spacing, and visual cadence**. The layout is part of the spell. The formatting, the glyphs, breath lines, and visual rhythm, serves a somatic function that cannot be fully replicated in standard digital formats.

However, we recognize that **print-first publishing creates real access barriers** for many readers, including blind/low-vision users, people who use screen readers, and those who cannot hold or purchase a physical copy.

This is not acceptable.

We are actively working to develop a **fully accessible digital version** that preserves the emotional and structural integrity of the work, without compromising the experience. This may include:

- **Screen-reader-compatible formatting**
- **Plain text alt versions** of each rite
- **Mp3 of all letters** in proper somatic cadence

For updates, visit:**www.invisible-grief.com/access** (You'll find resources, request forms, and alternate formats as they become available.)

If you have a question or access need that isn't addressed there, you're welcome to reach out via the site. Requests will be honored as capacity allows, and always with care.

A Note on Language, Systems, and Who Gets Left Out

This book was written in English. But grief isn't.

Grief speaks in silence. In gesture. In sighs. In mother tongues that never made it into textbooks. And yet, most resources are built for the fluent. The verbal. The documented. The system-trusted.

That's a failure. A systemic one. And I won't pretend otherwise.

Right now, this work is being carried by one pair of hands. There is no organization. No foundation. No translation team. Just me (and this book) trying to name the things most systems avoid.

But that doesn't mean we stop here.

This is the beginning of a larger body of work. One that *wants* to be translated, adapted, and held in more languages, more bodies, more realities than mine. And I am actively seeking the people who can help build that with integrity.

If you are someone with the skills, the reach, the lived experience to help open that door wider, **I welcome you.** Not as a volunteer. As a collaborator. A builder. A sacred co-carrier.

If you want to help expand this work across languages, abilities, formats, or continents, visit: www.invisible-grief.com and send me a message.

Companion Website (www.invisible-grief.com)

This book is a beginning, not a solution.

Grief doesn't follow a timeline. It doesn't respond to neat conclusions. And it rarely shows up in a way that lets itself be "finished."

Which is why this project doesn't end at the last page.

The *Invisible Grief of Adulthood* was created to name what hurts, but also to **support you** in the aftermath. The website exists to hold that space. To offer tools. To expand what's possible. To remind you that you're not doing this alone.

Some readers will use this book privately, picking it up and putting it down like a ritual object. Others will read it in community, at retreats, in therapy groups, in living rooms. Some will write their own letters. Some will share them. Some will never speak a word but still feel seen.

The website (www.invisible-grief.com) is here for all of that. And there is a QR code for direct access on the back cover.

It's where you'll find a growing repository containing:

- **Grief Atlas** eventually containing a supplemental packet for each letter. Packets discussing the themes and more.
- **Downloadables** for personal or group use
- **Letter-writing rituals** to help you move grief through the body
- A **quiet alcove for professionals** like therapists, educators, and grief workers
- And a **place to share your letter**, if you feel called to add your voice

This isn't extra content for the sake of content. It's part of the architecture. The digital companion to a sacred physical object.
An extended field of care.

So if something in this book opens you…go there.

Let it meet you where you are.

Let the grief move.

Let it name you back.

This space is evolving in real time. If you think a tool would be helpful and it is not available on the website. Feel free to reach out to me at sun@thehouseofthesun.com.

A Note on Process and Tools
This book was written by a single human.

Artificial intelligence was used as a support tool for editing, formatting, and organizing the manuscript. It did not generate the ideas, frameworks, or core content of this work.

Everything you're holding, from the structure, the voice, the system, is mine. Tools used include ChatGPT and Google Gemini.

Finally, these letters are for you.
For your healing, your reckoning, or whatever moment of life you're in. They weren't written to torch your life or fracture your relationships. They're not weapons. They're mirrors. If they invite you to reexamine what you've built, beautiful.

Share them with people you love and trust, or even a professional if you're working with a care team. **But don't use this book to cut others open without their consent.**

And if you find yourself sitting with a letter, unsure what to do next, go to the Return System that begins on page 397.

Prelude

Letter 0: To the One Wondering, "Why Invisible Grief"

Because not all grief
gets **named**.

Some of it arrives
without ceremony.

No funeral.
No diagnosis.
No clean narrative.

Just a quiet ache
that builds over time

in the breakroom,
in the shower,
in the middle of a conversation

where you smile
like nothing's wrong.

It's the grief
of becoming someone
you didn't mean
to become.

Of letting dreams
go quietly.
Of staying.
Of leaving.

Of waking up
one day

in a life
that technically works
but secretly **hurts**.

It's the grief of things
that didn't collapse loudly.

They just
eroded.

Piece
  by
    piece.

Until something inside you
stopped blooming.

That's ***invisible grief***.

It's not *less real*.
Not something you try to conceal
or maybe you do.

It's just
less
recognized.

These are the losses
that don't earn casseroles.

That no one checks in about.

That get folded
into your functioning

until no one
not even you
questions
the **cost**.

This book exists
to change that.

To say:

You're not crazy.
You're not weak.
You're not broken.

You're carrying things
that were never meant

to be
carried alone.

Grief doesn't need
a death certificate
to be valid.

If something inside you died
you get to
name it.

That's why ***invisible grief***.

Because what we don't name…
owns us.

And what we finally *see*
we can begin to
live with.
Or
live beyond.

If you're holding something *invisible*
this is your invitation
to ***name it***.

Now you see it.

–The Sun

4

Part I: The Quiet Room

This is where it begins.
Not with a crisis
but with that faint hum in your chest that whispers,
"This can't be all there is."

Nothing's technically wrong.
You're doing everything right.
You're performing adulthood like a pro:
answering emails, buying groceries, managing expectations.

But something's leaking.
And the leak is starting to sound like your real voice.

This is grief with good posture
the kind that folds itself into routines.
The kind that lets you function,
but quietly strips the color out of your days.

This is where people stay for years.
Not because it's safe.
But because it's familiar.
Because naming the ache would mean
changing everything.

These letters live in that room.
The one with no visible damage
but hairline fractures snaking through every wall.

This isn't your breakdown.
It's the moment you realize:
you've been living someone else's life in your own body.

Letter 1: To the One Who Feels Like They're Failing at Being an Adult

You pay your bills.
You answer texts.
You show up.

You smile
when someone asks
how you're doing,

even though the real answer
would take too long
and scare them.

You're doing everything right
and it still feels like
you're falling apart.

But not dramatically.
Just...
slowly.

A quiet erosion
of joy.

A soft, constant dread.

Like you're being smothered
by your own life
and no one notices.

You think the problem is you.

That maybe if you had better
habits,
more discipline,
a morning routine

you'd feel okay.

But let me tell you the truth
you already know
in your bones:

**The version of adulthood
you're trying to live
was built on a lie.**

It sold you a checklist:
Career.
Partner.
Mortgage.
401(k).

And whispered that
if you followed it,
you'd feel alive.

But what it didn't say
is that the cost of that checklist
might be your soul.

You were told to trade your time
for **money**.

Your instincts
for **obedience**.

Your curiosity
for **productivity**.

Your body
for **performance**.

Your relationships
for **status**.

Your weekends
for **recovery**.

And when the joy
started leaking out of you,
they told you to:

✓ meditate
✓ take a bubble bath
✓ journal your gratitude

for a life
that doesn't
feel like yours.

No wonder you feel like you're failing.

But what if you're not?

What if this ache you carry
isn't dysfunction
but a sign
of your refusal
to fully disappear?

What if the part of you
that's breaking down
is the part that still
knows the truth?

That it's not supposed
to be this hard.

That life was meant to be
more than logistics
and debt
and digital fatigue.

**That success without
aliveness
is just another kind of death.**

You are not failing
to be an adult.

You are resisting
a version of adulthood
that asks you to betray yourself
every day
and call it maturity.

That resistance?
That's your aliveness,
fighting to survive.

So let it.

Let yourself grieve
the version of life
you were promised.

Let yourself say,
"This isn't it."

Let yourself be angry.
Let yourself want more.
Let yourself stop pretending.

Because the truth is:
you were never meant
to wear a costume every day
just to be taken seriously.

You were meant to live
messy,
radiant,
unoptimized,
and free.

So if you can't keep performing
this version of adulthood?

Good.

Let it crack.
Let it fall apart.

That's not your failure.
That's your threshold.

You're not broken.
You're waking up.

—The Sun

Letter 2: To the One Who Thought Adulthood Would Come With Instructions

You kept waiting
for someone to explain it.

The rules.
The rhythm.
The moment when
it would all make sense.

When you'd feel like you
belonged in your life
instead of just **surviving** it.

You watched the grown-ups
when you were young
they seemed so sure.

Bills paid.
Groceries bought.
Mornings managed
like clockwork.

You thought:
They must know something
I don't.

Some secret.
Some system.
Some manual
passed down
behind closed doors.

But when it became your turn
when your name
was on the lease,

when your phone
was the one that rang
in emergencies,

when no one else
was coming to fix it
you realized the truth:

There is **no manual**.

There are no real grown-ups.
Just people with decent
credit scores
and **complicated grief**.

No one tells you
that the to-do list never ends.

That your body will ache
in places
you don't have names for.

That **joy takes effort** now.

That you'll sometimes look
at your life and think:
Is this really it?

No one tells you
how **lonely** it can be
to carry everything
without anyone noticing.

How hard it is to admit
that you don't know
what the hell you're doing
even after all these years
of pretending you do.

So let me say it plain:

You are not behind.
You are not broken.

You're just an adult
in a world
that never gave you a **map**.

And yet, somehow
you've kept going.

Even when it didn't make sense.
Even when you were afraid.
Even when the systems failed you,
the people disappointed you,
and your dreams shrunk
to fit your reality.

You **kept going**.

And that matters
more than anyone says.

So maybe there's no one coming
to hand you the instructions.

But there is this:

You are not the only one
who feels lost.

You are not the only one
who whispers *"I'm tired"*
while brushing your teeth.

You are not the only one
who wonders
if you missed the memo.

There was **no memo**.

Just us.
Stumbling forward.
Still here.
Still trying.

And that's
enough.

–**The Sun**

Letter 3: To the One Who Can't Keep Wearing the Costume of Adulthood

You wake up
and put it on.

The calm face.
The composed voice.
The plan for the day.

You nod at the calendar
like you're ready.
Like your bones didn't
scream getting out of bed.

You do what they said to do.
You make the calls.
You pay the bill.
You answer the emails

like any of it
means anything.

You're not failing.
You're performing.
And you're tired.

Because somewhere along the way,
"being an adult" stopped
meaning freedom
and started meaning
being fine with being:

exhausted
overworked
under-touched
under-seen

and told you're lucky
to have a job.

They gave you a script:
Be responsible.

Be productive.
Be realistic.
Be grateful.
Be reachable.
Be nice.

What they meant was:
Be numb.

And you tried.
God, you tried.

You played the part.
You got the job,
or the degree,
or the relationship,
or the apartment
with the dishwasher.

You filled out the forms.
You showed up
when you didn't want to.
You said "it's fine"
when it wasn't.

And now you're standing
in a life you built
to survive

wondering why it feels
like a costume
that never fit.

You are not broken.
You're just choking
on the lie.

The lie
that adulthood means
giving up wonder.

The lie
that safety matters more than aliveness.

The lie
that you are only as valuable
as what you produce.

That grief you're carrying?

**It's the grief
of living inside a life
that never made room
for your soul.**

So here's the truth:
You don't have to keep wearing it.

You can take it off.

The calm voice.
The bulletproof plan.
The "I've got this" mask
that's cracking at the edges.

You don't need
to burn it all down.

But you do need
to tell the truth.

You're not okay
pretending anymore.

And that's not weakness.

That's your life
asking to finally begin.

—The Sun

Letter 4: To the One Who's Still Trying to Earn Their Place in a System They Secretly Hate

You know it's broken.

The jobs.
The housing.
The fake friendships
and empty praise.
The grind.
The rules that change
depending on who's watching.

You know it.

You see through it.
You make jokes about it.
You repost the memes.

You say all the right things about
capitalism,
burnout,
emotional labor,
productivity,
politics.

But even still

some part of you
still wants in.

Some part of you still hopes
you'll finally be picked.

**That your inbox
will hold good news.**

**That your brilliance
will be discovered.**

**That your hard work
will be rewarded.**

That someone will tell you:

"You did it.
You made it.
You belong."

And maybe
that's the sharpest grief of all.

**Knowing it's all rigged
and still bending yourself
to be worthy inside it.**

You don't need a reminder
that the system is cruel.

You already know that.

What you need
is someone to name
the quiet war
happening inside you.

The one where you resent the machine
but still measure your worth
by its metrics.

The one where you want out
but still fantasize
about being chosen.

The one where you judge yourself
for craving validation
from the very structures
that have ignored you,
exploited you,
reduced you

again
and again.

So let's name it clean:

You are not weak

for wanting in.
You are not stupid
for still hoping to be seen.

You are not a hypocrite
for craving the dream
you know is a lie.

You were raised inside it.
Fed on its myths.

Taught that
love comes after achievement.

Taught that
safety comes after compliance.

Taught that
success will save you.

And now?

You're awake.

Which means every rejection
stings twice.

Not just because
you were passed over
but because you knew
it wouldn't save you,
and still…

you hoped.

So let this be your unburdening.

You're not crazy.
You're not lost.
You're not behind.

You are in
a sacred
in-between.

No longer asleep
but not yet free.

And the ache you feel?

**It's not failure.
It's your soul shedding
what was never yours to carry.**

Let yourself grieve it.
Let yourself want more than scraps.
Let yourself feel the burn
of wanting in
while walking out.

You're not broken.

You're just waking up
in a world
that makes sanity
look like rebellion.

Let it burn.

And let it be holy.

—The Sun

Letter 5: To the One Who Always Has to Prove Their Worth Through Doing

You never felt safe
just being.

So you became
a weaponized tenderness.
A readiness.
A résumé.
A living
logistical system.

You learned how to
anticipate.
You learned how to
disappear.

You call it love
but it's always been
performance.

You
who keeps the machine running
even when your chest is folding in.
You
who shows up with answers
when your own mouth is dry
from sobbing.
You
who wipes the counter clean
while praying
someone
asks
if you're okay.

Let's stop pretending.
You are not helpful.

You are holy scaffolding.
And they will climb you
until your bones give out

**then call you lazy
for collapsing.**

They don't see you.
They see:
a function.
A task rabbit.
A mother.
A martyr.

And god,
you've made it look easy.

You don't get rest.
You get
applause.

You don't get love.
You get
used.

And you take it
because being wanted for your gifts
feels better
than not being wanted
at all.

So you do.
And do.
And do.
Until there's nothing left
but an echo
wearing your face.

You were never taught
how to be adored in stillness.
Only tolerated
in exhaustion.

Let me ruin the lie.
Let me say the thing
that breaks the ritual
you were raised inside.

**You don't owe the world
a single fucking thing.**

Not your effort.
Not your excellence.
Not your performance.

You are not scaffolding.
You are not a productivity report.
You are not
what survives the fire
to rebuild someone else's house.

You are a soul.

**And you are allowed
to sit down.**

Like a god.

Without permission.
Without apology.
Without collapse.

Let the dishes rot.
Let the to-do list burn.
Let the room fall silent
while you breathe
and do
absolutely
nothing.

You are not a utility.
You are the altar.

And if they leave
when you stop performing
they were praying
to your usefulness,
not to you.

Take one day.
One hour.
One minute

where you do not earn
your existence.

And when the shame comes?

Don't flinch.
Stand still
and let it pass
like a storm
you no longer need to explain.

You are not more lovable
because you ache.
You are not more worthy
because you endure.
You are not more real
because you perform collapse
with grace.

You're allowed
to be radiant
and still.

You're allowed
to be sacred
and unapologetically idle.

**You're allowed
to be loved
when you're not
doing a goddamn thing.**

You're allowed
to be.

Just
be.

You.

—The Sun

Letter 6: To the One Whose Productivity Is Slowly Killing Them

You're the one
they count on.

The first to say yes.
The last to rest.

You get it done
even if it guts you.

You push through
even when your body
begs you to stop.

They call you a machine.
High-functioning.
Driven.
Unstoppable.

And part of you
wears that like a crown.

Because somewhere along the way,
you were taught to mistake:
exhaustion for excellence.
overextension for value.
output for worth.

But let's tell the truth:

You're tired
in a way sleep doesn't touch.

Your to-do list
has a to-do list.

And the more you accomplish,
the more invisible you feel.

You don't know how to stop.
Because stopping feels like failure.

And slowing down
feels like disappearing.

Because if you're not useful
what are you?

You've forgotten how to be anything
but efficient.

But love, you were never built
to live like a spreadsheet.

To be optimized.
To be harvestable.

To be a walking proof
of productivity.

You are not
a quarterly report.

You are not
your inbox.

**You are not
a performance metric
for a system
that never once asked
how your soul is doing.**

You are a person.

And you are allowed
to want rest.

Not earned rest
real rest.

The kind that comes
before collapse.

The kind that comes
without guilt.

I know you think the world
will fall apart
if you don't keep holding it.

But maybe the real collapse
is happening inside you

every time you pretend
you're okay
just to keep things moving.

So here's your permission:

You can stop.
You can slow down.

You can choose yourself
before the world asks
for another piece.

Because what good is a life
that's impressive on paper
but uninhabitable in practice?

You don't need
another productivity hack.

**You need to come home
to the parts of you
that never cared
about being efficient**

only real.
Only whole.
Only alive.

Let that be enough.

—The Sun

Letter 7: To the One Who's Exhausted From Holding It All Together

You're so tired.
But it's the kind of tired
that doesn't sleep off.

It's the kind of tired
that builds silently.

From smiling
when you want to scream.

From fixing everything
before it breaks.

From carrying the weight
of everyone else's comfort
like your sanity depends on it.

Because maybe
it does.

Because if you stop moving
if you stop:
• caring
• cooking
• correcting
• replying
• managing
• absorbing

what happens?
Does it all fall apart?

Do you?

You don't get to fall apart.
You're the one
people count on.

The one who always knows
the date,

the time,
the place,
the bill,
the answer.

The one who swallows your needs
to keep the peace.
The one who makes it all
look effortless
even when your soul
is threadbare.

And no one knows.
Because you don't let them.

Because when they ask
how you're doing,
you say:
"I'm okay."

Because saying:
"I'm drowning"
feels like an inconvenience.

But love
this is not what strength
was meant to look like.

You've built a life
by being unshakable.
But somewhere in there,
you forgot
that you're a person too.

A person with limits.

A person who shouldn't have to
bleed quietly
just to make other people
comfortable.

Let me be the one
to say it:

You are not lazy.
You are not weak.
You are not failing.

You are tired
because you've been in overdrive
for years.

You are tired
because this world rewards burnout
and calls it "grit."

You are tired
because you never learned
how to be held
only how to hold.

But you're allowed to stop.

Even just for a moment.
Let the laundry sit.
Let the texts go unanswered.
Let the mask slip.

Nothing bad will happen
if you fall apart.

And even if it does
you will still be here.
Loved.
Held.
Human.

This isn't about giving up.

It's about laying down
the burden

of holding everything together

just so no one else
has to feel discomfort.
You're allowed
to let it be messy.

You're allowed
to let someone else
carry you.

You don't have to earn rest.

You don't have to prove pain.

You don't have to stay strong
just because you always have.

Come lay it down.

Even just for today.

Let the world spin
without you.

It knows how.

You've done enough.

–The Sun

Letter 8: To the One Who Can't Tell If They're Resting or Numbing

You're tired.
Not just sleepy
spent.

Soul-tired.
That bone-deep exhaustion
that doesn't go away with a nap.

So you cancel.
You stay in.
You scroll.

You watch the same shows,
eat the same meals,
say the same things:
"I'm just resting."
"I'm giving myself grace."
"I need a break."

And maybe you do.
God knows this world
wrings people dry
and then calls it "balance."

But if you're honest?
There's a part of you
that isn't sure.

Because the rest
doesn't feel restorative.
It feels slippery.
It feels like disappearing.
It feels like you're trying
to fall asleep
inside your own life
and hoping no one notices.

You are not lazy.
You are not weak.
You are not broken.

But you might be numbing.
Because rest and numbing
can wear the same clothes.
They can both
look like stillness.

But only one feeds you.
The other just
freezes the hunger.

Real rest
softens you
back into yourself.
It makes space.
It invites breath.

Numbing
puts everything on mute
and tells you that peace
is just silence
with better branding.

So how do you know the difference?

Ask yourself this:
Do I feel more **alive**
when I come back?
Or do I still feel
foggy,
brittle,
disconnected?

Does this stillness
hold me…
…or just hide me?

Because there's nothing wrong
with needing a break.

But some breaks
become exits.

Some "days off"

become doorways
we never return from.

And you don't need
to perform productivity
to be valid
but you also don't need
to go so still
that you forget
what movement feels like.

You are allowed
to rest.
You are allowed
to pause.

But don't mistake
sedation for sanctuary.

You're not wrong
for wanting to disappear sometimes.

The world is heavy.

But you're still here.
Which means
part of you
still wants in.

So take the bath.
Take the nap.
Take the break.
And then
come back.

Not because you have to.
But because you can.

Because numbness is a cocoon
but rest
is a rebirth.

–The Sun

Letter 9: To the One Whose Life Always Costs More Than It Pays

You're doing everything right.

You show up.
You try hard.
You care.

You manage what's expected
even when no one sees
what it takes out of you.

And still
you're exhausted.

Not the kind of tired
that a nap fixes.

The kind that sits in your bones.
The kind that makes you wonder
how long you can keep
going like this.

Because no matter
how carefully you budget
your money,
your energy,
your time

it never adds up.

You give
more than you get.

You hustle
and compromise
and accommodate

and somehow
you're still in emotional debt.

The rent is paid,
but your joy is bankrupt.

You've mastered surviving,
but you haven't felt alive
in months.

You're rich in responsibility
and poor in rest.

And the world keeps telling you
it's your fault.

You should manage better.
Think more positively.
Be more grateful.
Try harder.

But let's be clear:

You are not the problem.
You are not broken.

You are not lazy.
You are not doing life wrong.

You're just trapped
in a system
that only rewards
the visible.

That measures worth
in output.

That dangles ease
like a prize for those
who "deserve" it

as if being human
didn't already earn you
that right.

This life
shouldn't be a spreadsheet

where love,
joy,
and freedom
are luxuries
you're expected to earn
after everything else is done.

You don't need more willpower.
You need relief.

You need help without shame.
Rest without guilt.
Support
without having to prove
how bad it's gotten.

You don't need a better routine.

You need a life that gives back.

A life
that doesn't drain your soul
just to keep the lights on.

So if you're waiting for permission
this is it.

Say "no" more often.

Quit the thing
that's bleeding you dry.

Ask for the help
you've been quietly wishing
someone would offer.

Leave the job
that's killing you.
Or don't

but stop pretending
it's fine.

Because you're not meant
to survive your life.

You're meant
to live it.

And any system,
relationship,
or story
that only ever takes from you
was never sacred enough
to stay.

You're allowed
to want a life
that actually feeds you back.

Not eventually.

Not after you've earned it.

Now.

—The Sun

Letter 10: To the One Living in the Body That Survival Built

You didn't ask
for this version of you.

But here it is:

The weight
you didn't consent to.

The scars
you didn't vote for.

The brain fog,
the stretch marks,
the pain
that pulses through joints
once agile.

The soft armor
that showed up to protect you
and never left.

**This body
is not the one
from the before.**

Before the trauma.
Before the illness.
Before the medication
that saved you
but also took something.

Maybe you mourn
what you used to be able to do.

Or wear.

Or feel.

Maybe you hate
that you're still negotiating
with mirrors.

Or bracing for comments.

Or trying to convince yourself
it's not your fault.

And it's not.

You are not lazy.
You are not weak.
You are not a failure.

You are a survivor.

And this body?

It's proof.

Proof that you stayed.
That you endured.
That you walked through hell
and kept going

even if you crawled.

You don't have to love it today.

But maybe,
for now,
you can say:

Thank you.

And let that
be enough.

—The Sun

Letter 11: To the One Whose Body Changed Without Warning

You used to trust your body.
Now it feels like a stranger.

The sleep stopped
helping.

The pain showed up
uninvited.

The weight
changed.

The energy
disappeared.

The hunger
came and went
without logic.

No crash.
No dramatic injury.
Just a slow,
quiet betrayal.

And when you tried to name it
they told you to:
• drink more water
• get more steps
• manifest better health
• stop complaining
• be grateful

But you remember
what it felt like
to move without pain.
To run.
To fuck.
To dance.
To wake up
without doing math

on what you'd
have to cancel
just to make it
through the day.

You've mourned
in silence.

You've Googled things
you never thought you'd Google.

You've gone to war
with your reflection.

You've bargained with yourself:
in dressing rooms,
in doctors' offices,
in the mirror.

Here's what no one says:
You are not broken.
You are in transition.
And it is not your fault.

Bodies are not static.
They are not obedient.
They are not machines.
They are:
mess,
miracle,
mystery,
memory.

And even now
when it hurts,
when it's hard
your body is still yours.
Still trying.
Still carrying you.
Still asking to be loved.

You don't have to wait
until it changes again
to be kind to it.

You don't have to perform gratitude
to be allowed to grieve.
You get to name this loss.
You get to stay tender.

–The Sun

Letter 12: To the One Who Doesn't Feel Anything (And Is Starting to Worry That They Should)

You thought this book
would break you open.

But here you are.

Dry-eyed.

Blank.

Still scrolling.

Still waiting
for the feeling to come.

This letter is not here
to shame you.
It's here
to witness you.

Because numbness
is not the absence of grief.
It's often the evidence of it.

You did what you had to do
to survive.
You built a house of:
logic
distance
control.

And it worked.
But it's lonely, isn't it?

To watch the world cry
and not know how.

To feel like you're locked
behind glass
even from yourself.

To read
line after line after line
and still not know
where it hurts.

Let this be the first crack.
Not a breakthrough.
Just a whisper.

You are not broken.
You are just buried.

And even frost
thaws
when the Sun
stays
long enough.

With you,
The Sun

Letter 13: To the One Who's Afraid There's Nothing Truly Special About Them

You've been quietly waiting
your whole life
for someone to tell you
that you are extraordinary.

Not because you want to be famous.
Not because you think you're better.

But because some part of you
has never really believed
that being yourself
is enough
to make someone stop in their tracks
and see you.

So you perform.

Just a little.

You read the room.

You sharpen your edges
or soften your voice
depending on what they need.

You're likable.
You're smart.
You're a great listener.

**But you don't feel
unforgettable.**

And that's the wound, Isn't it?

You think your presence
doesn't linger.
That if people walked away,
you'd be replaced in an instant.

That your name
doesn't echo
in anyone's chest
when you're not around.

So, you overcompensate.

You show up big.
You give the best advice.
You remember birthdays.
You do the work
to be lovable.

But it still feels
like you're borrowing
someone else's light
just to be seen.

So let me speak the thing
plainly:

You are not invisible.

You are not generic.

You are not just
"nice" or "helpful" or "solid."

You are singular.

And the tragedy
is that no one ever really told you
with the kind of conviction
that sinks in
and stays.

So hear it now,
clean and clear:

You don't need a bigger story.
You don't need a hidden talent.
You don't need a spiritual glow-up.

You, as you are,
already carry a frequency
the world has never seen before.

You don't need to try harder.

You need to come home.

To your quirks.
To your longings.
To the things you do
when no one's watching.
To the laugh that escapes
when you forget to be self-conscious.

That is the spark.
That is the echo.
That is the thing that makes someone
not just notice you
but remember you.

You don't have to wait for proof.

You are the proof.

And when you stop
trying to be special

you'll finally feel
how deeply
you already are.

—The Sun

Letter 14: To the One Who Keeps Getting "Close" But Never All the Way In

You're almost always there.

In the room.
In the text thread.
In the job interview.
In the relationship
that nearly becomes something real.

You're inches from arrival
but something always
stops
     just short
         of landing.

You're told you're impressive.
You're told you're valuable.
You're told you're
"almost exactly what we're looking for."

But somehow
they choose someone else.

The friend group never really opens.
The lover stays distant.
The promotion goes to the person
who didn't even want it
(or didn't try as hard as you did).

And you're left asking:
What am I doing wrong?

You're not imagining it.
There is a pattern.

A quiet repetition
of almosts.
Of waiting rooms.
Of doorways
that never fully
open.

And the worst part is
you started to believe it.

Maybe you're not it.
Not lovable enough.
Not cool enough.
Not seamless enough to slide in.

So you adjust.
You shape-shift.
You soften your edges.
You try to become
whatever would finally
let you in.

But the truth is
they never saw you.

They were drawn to your glow,
but not ready
for your heat.

You were never
almost enough.

You were
too much
for people
still afraid
of their own fire.

Still choosing comfort
over truth.
Still clinging to the familiar
instead of the real.

This isn't about effort.
It's about refusal.

Refusal to keep
auditioning
for rooms
that were never built
to hold you.

You're not meant to be invited.
You're meant
to blaze
your own threshold
into being.

Stop twisting.
Stop dimming.
Stop shrinking.

You're not a maybe.
You're not a backup plan.
You're not someone's runner-up.

You are the thing.
The match.
The altar.
The burn.

And the ones who are meant
to hold you fully
won't need convincing.

They'll walk through fire
to find you.

—The Sun

Letter 15: To the One Who Got Everything They Wanted…and Still Feels Nothing

You did it.
You built the life.
Checked the boxes.
Crossed the finish line.

You got the job,
the partner,
the house,
the title.

People say,
"You're so lucky."

And you smile and say,
"I know."

But inside?
There's just… **silence**.

A blankness
you can't explain.
A numb hum
behind the eyes.

You stand in the
middle of your life
like a guest who
showed up early
to a party that
never started.

**This was supposed
to feel different.**

The success.
The stability.
The structure.

You thought you'd finally feel full.

But instead,
you feel like a well-decorated room
no one lives in.

Empty in velvet.

You wonder if you're broken.
Ungrateful.
Spoiled.

You try to snap yourself out of it:
Gratitude journals.
Podcasts.
Peloton.

But the void
doesn't care about your affirmations.

Because here's the truth
no one talks about:

**You can do everything right
and still end up wrong.**

You can follow every rule
and still feel lost.

You can build a "good life"
and still have a soul
that feels caged.

Not because you failed.
But because this version of success
wasn't designed for your aliveness.

It was designed for obedience.
For optics.
For applause
that never touches the inside.

**Your emptiness isn't a flaw.
It's an alarm.**

A quiet rebellion
inside your bones.

Something in you
is still trying to breathe
under the weight of the life
you thought you had to want.

So listen.

Not to your schedule.
Not to your performance metrics.

To the ache.
To the whisper.
To the part of you
that keeps saying:

There has to be more than this.

Because there is.

But you won't find it
by running harder
in the same direction.

You'll find it
when you start
telling the truth.

Start there.

Even if your voice shakes.
Even if it undoes everything
they told you success should look like.
Even if you disappoint
the people who loved
the version of you
that never said "no".

This is your life.

Not your résumé.
Not your brand.

Not your curated feed
of "should be happy" snapshots.

And you deserve
to feel alive inside it.

Fully.
Fiercely.
For real.

Burn the blueprint.

There's something better
waiting in the ash.

—The Sun

Letter 16: To the One Who Thinks Peace Is Boring Because They've Only Known Chaos

Stillness makes you twitchy,
doesn't it?

Quiet makes you
scan the room for threats.

Love without tension
feels suspicious.

A day without crisis
feels... *wrong*.

You say you want peace.
You say you're tired.
You say you're ready
to stop fighting everything.

But when peace shows up,
you start reaching
for the emergency brake.

Because you were built in chaos.

You learned to read the weather
in people's moods.
You learned to move fast,
stay sharp,
never relax.

You learned that safety
isn't a given
it's a performance.

You became a master of crisis.
The fixer.
The calm-in-the-storm.
The one who handles shit.

But now?
Now the storm has passed.

And you're left
with a silence
that feels too loud.

And here's the truth
you may not want to hear:

You don't know how to feel safe
without a threat.
You don't know how to rest
without guilt.
You don't know how to receive
without a plan to repay it.

Peace isn't boring.
It's just unfamiliar.

And unfamiliar feels dangerous
when your nervous system
was raised in fire.

So when the good thing feels dull?
When the calm feels like
something must be wrong?

When your body itches
to create friction
where there is none?

Pause.

You're not broken.
You're just **detoxing**
from a lifetime of emergency.

This isn't about shame.
It's about recognition.

Of how much of your "drive"
was really just survival.
Of how much of your "independence"
was really just no one showing up.
Of how much of your "resilience"

was just being too scared
to fall apart.

But you don't need to
live like that now.

You don't have to
manufacture drama
just to feel alive.

You don't have to sabotage softness
because you don't trust it'll stay.

Let yourself adjust.
To slow mornings.
To kind people.
To not being in charge
of every fire.

To love that doesn't hurt.

Because peace isn't boring.
It's **holy.**

And it will feel like nothing at first
because your body has never known a life
that didn't ask it
to brace.

But keep breathing.
Keep staying.
Let the boredom come.
Let the quiet land.

And one day,
you'll realize it's not emptiness.

It's **ease**.

And you were always allowed
to want that.

—**The Sun**

Letter 17: To The One Who's Angry All The Time

You don't wake up mad.
Not always.

But

by the time the
coffee's cold,
by the time the
third email hits,
by the time
the wrong tone
comes out of someone's mouth

there it is.

The heat.
The edge.
The tightness in your jaw
that's older
than whatever just happened.

You're not just angry.
You're saturated.

And maybe no one ever told you this,
but anger is often
grief in armor.

Not just the grief of death
or breakups
but the slow-drip grief
of unmet needs.

The **grief** of being the one
who always holds it together.

The **grief** of having
no room to collapse.

The **grief** of being misunderstood.

The **grief** of carrying more
than your share
for too long.

You think you're losing it.
You're not.

Your body is ringing the alarm
for a grief
you haven't had time to name.

Maybe it's sadness.
Maybe it's loneliness.

Maybe it's the crushing,
constant pressure
of trying to be good,
be strong, be fine.
But it's not just rage.

It's something **sacred**
trying to get out.

Let that be the beginning.

And let's be clear:

This is not a free pass to lash out.

This is not permission
to leak your grief
onto everyone around you
and call it healing.

This is a call
to take responsibility
for what's trying to surface.

To grieve
what's underneath the anger
without turning it
into someone else's burden.

You're not broken.
You're **backed up.**

And the anger?
That's just the grief,
knocking louder.

—The Sun

Letter 18: To the One Who's Tired of Being Strong All the Time

You don't get to fall apart,
do you?

Not really.

Not without consequences.
Not without someone needing
something from you
five minutes later.

You're the one
who knows what to say.
The one who keeps it moving.
The one who picks up the pieces.
The one who always seems to have room.

You've made it a lifestyle
being okay enough for everyone else.

But you're not okay.
Not really.
Not all the way.

You're tired.

Of holding it.
Of hiding it.
Of hauling a world
that never stops needing you.

Because here's the unspoken trap
of being "strong":

People start to believe

you don't need.
That you don't break.
That you don't bleed.

They come to you like a well.

But who fills you?

And maybe you've tried.

To whisper the truth.
To say you're overwhelmed.
To name the ache
you wake up with.

But it never seems to land.
Or it gets minimized.
Or someone needs you
even while you're trying to unravel.

So you keep it quiet.

You call it "just being tired."

You pour a drink.

You scroll until the feelings go fuzzy.

You laugh it off and say,
"It's fine, I've got it."

But part of you wants to scream:

No. I don't got it.
I'm not okay.
I'm carrying too much.
And I need someone
to hold me
for once.

Let me be that someone.

Let this be the space.

To collapse
without being asked for anything.
To soften
without being punished.
To be human
not heroic.

You don't have to earn rest.

You don't have to prove
your pain is real.

You don't have to make it palatable
so others will accept it.

Your exhaustion is evidence.

Of care.
Of effort.
Of showing up.

Not of failure.

So if all you can do today
is exhale?

Exhale.

If all you want is to cry
and not explain it?

Cry.

If the strongest thing you do
is not push through?

That is enough.

You are allowed
to put it down.

And if no one else says it

I'm proud of you.

Not for how much
you carry,
but for daring
to say:

"I can't keep carrying it like this."

That's strength too.
The kind that saves your life.

—The Sun

Letter 19: To the One Who Gave Up a Dream Because Life Didn't Leave Room

You didn't quit
because you didn't care.

You didn't stop
because you weren't good enough.

You didn't let go
because you lacked
discipline,
or drive,
or some mystical quality
the "successful" people
seem to have in endless supply.

You let go
because something had to give.

And it was you.

Rent was due.
Someone needed you.
You didn't have
the connections.
Or the time.
Or the stamina
to keep grinding
toward something
that always stayed
just out of reach.

And even now
after the decision,
after the silence,
after the part of you
that held the dream
went still

there's still
a quiet ache
when you think about it.

You see someone else doing it,
and your chest tightens.

Not with jealousy.
With recognition.

You think:
That could've been me.

And then
Maybe it was never meant to be.

But that second part?
That's not truth.
That's survival.

Because the real truth
is messier.

It wasn't a lack of talent.
It wasn't a lack of will.
**It was the math of a life
that kept asking for more
than you had to give.**

And eventually
you said,
I can't.

And there's no shame in that.

But let's also not lie
about what it cost.

It cost
a piece of you.

A version of you
that still believed
in possibility.

A version
that whispered,
What if?

A version
that moved through the world
with a secret shine
because something holy
lived inside your chest
and wanted out.

You didn't bury that dream
because it didn't matter.

You buried it
because you didn't
have the oxygen
to keep it alive.

But maybe it's still in there.

Not for resurrection.
Not to pick up
where you left off.

But to grieve.

To name what was lost.
To tell the truth
about what it meant.
To finally give it
the ceremony
it never got.

You don't have to revive it.

But you do deserve
to mourn it.

Because your dream was real.
And it mattered.
And so do you.

—The Sun

Letter 20: To the One Who Forgot What They Even Like Anymore

You used to know.

What made you laugh.
What made you ache
in the best way.

What made the world feel
like a playground
instead of a punishment.

You used to follow whims.
You used to waste time.
You used to want things
without needing to justify them.

But now?

You scroll.
You respond.
You survive.

You stare at the weekend
and feel nothing.

You try to answer the question,
"What do you want?"
and come up blank.

Because somewhere along the way,
you outsourced
your preferences
to performance.

You traded
your delight for discipline.

You confused
being "easygoing"
with disappearing.

And no one noticed.

Because you're so good at fitting in.
So good at supporting
everyone else's dream.
So good at making life work.

But here's the grief no one names:

**You can make it all work
and still feel like
you're not living your life.**

Because it's not your life
if it has no trace of you in it.

So let's start small.

Let's remember.

Not with pressure.
Not with another

self-improvement checklist.

With curiosity.

What did you love
before the world got loud?

What did you reach for
before someone told you it was
stupid,
childish,
unrealistic,
indulgent?

What makes your body
hum?

What makes you lose track of
time?

What makes you feel
not useful, not productive,
but real?

Don't aim for joy.

Aim for a flicker.
A spark.
A maybe.

Try the song.
Take the detour.
Touch the color.
Say no to the thing that flattens you.

This isn't about becoming someone new.
It's about becoming someone true.

You didn't lose yourself.

**You buried yourself
under years of pleasing,
performing,
and pretending not to care.**

So dig.

You're still in there.
And your life misses you.

—The Sun

Letter 21: To the One Who Knows the Grief Is Coming

You feel it
before it arrives.

The tremble in the air.
The slant of the light.
The way ordinary things
suddenly shimmer
with goodbye.

Maybe no one around you knows.
Maybe it hasn't even happened yet.

But your body does.
Your heart does.

You are living
in the between-space

where the world keeps spinning,
but something in you
has already started
letting go.

There's a name for this:
anticipatory grief.

It's the ache
that doesn't wait for permission.

The sorrow
that builds a nest in your chest
before there's a reason
anyone else can see.

And it's real.
It counts.
It matters.

You might feel guilty.
Or dramatic.

Or like you're grieving
too soon.

But timing
doesn't matter
to the soul.

It knows what's coming.

And it's bracing
the only way it knows how
by beginning
to mourn
now.

This isn't weakness.

It's preparation.

It's a form of love.

You don't have to justify the weight.
You don't have to explain
your preemptive ache.
You don't even have to be ready.

You just have to be honest:

This hurts.
Even now.
Even before.

And you're allowed
to say so.

—The Sun

Letter 22: To the One Who Thought Healing Would Feel Better

You thought it
would be lighter by now.

Cleaner.
Brighter.
Easier.

You thought that
doing the work
would bring peace.

Not… this.

Not the rawness.
Not the holy confusion.
Not the moments
where you're more awake
but somehow
lonelier too.

You gave up the coping mechanisms.
You stopped pretending.
You told the truth.
You walked away.

You did the thing
that was supposed
to make it all worth it.

And now?
You're just here.

Sober
in a world
that still wants you sedated.

Present
in a life
that still isn't quite built
for the real you.

No one tells you this part.
That healing isn't a glow-up.

It's a demolition.

It's sitting
in the ruins of who you were
with no blueprint
for who comes next.

It's crying in your car.
Ghosting social events.
Lying on the floor
wondering
if you just made everything worse.

You thought
healing would feel like love.

But sometimes
it feels like **loss**.

Loss of who you used to be.
Loss of illusions
that used to protect you.
Loss of relationships
that could only love the mask.

But this pain?
It's not proof
you're doing it wrong.

**It's proof
that you're finally telling the truth.**

And the truth is sharp
before it's soft.

It guts you
before it grounds you.

It wrecks your performance
so your soul
can finally enter the room.

So if you're sitting
in the rubble

I just want to say:

I see you.

No, it doesn't feel good right now.
But **feeling**
is good.

It means you're here.
It means you stayed.
It means you chose life
even when it didn't clap for you.

You're not broken.
You're becoming.

Not the glossy version.
Not the Instagram version.

The real one.

The one who
doesn't have to fake peace
to be lovable.

The one who
can hold chaos and beauty
in the same breath.

The one who
no longer needs to be understood
to be whole.

You're not behind.
You're not crazy.
You're not alone.

You're healing.

And sometimes?
That just hurts.

But it's still sacred.

—The Sun

Letter 23: To the One Who Got Scorched By Someone Else's Fire

You didn't ask for this.
You didn't light the match.
You didn't write the lie.
You didn't twist the story,
or break the promise,
or gamble with someone else's heart.

You were just there.
Trusting.
Building.
Hoping.

And then one day
boom.

There it was.

The moment you realized
they were never going to be the person
you kept making excuses for.

That's the grief
no one talks about.

The grief
of realizing your hope was holy
but you handed it
to someone
who couldn't carry it.

And now?

Now you walk around
with smoke in your lungs
and a quiet rage in your chest,

because no one warned you
how much it would hurt
to mourn something
that was already burning

while you were still
trying to build a home.

You didn't fuck around.
But you sure as hell
found out.

So here's what I want to say:

You're allowed to be angry.

You're allowed to miss them
and still know
they were wrong for you.

You're allowed to grieve
the version of them
they never became.

You're allowed to walk away
and still wonder
what would've happened
if they had just grown.

But more than anything?

You're allowed to rebuild.

Without apology.
Without explanation.
Without needing their permission.

Let their fire make you
sharper.

Not smaller.
Not colder.

Sharper.

Because some people
don't wake up
until the house
is already ash.

But you

you're still here.

And now
you get to decide
who walks through your doors next.

—The Sun

Letter 24: To the One Who Was Never Allowed to Fall Apart

You were the strong one.
The dependable one.
The one who held it together
when everyone else
fell apart.

Even as a kid
you could feel
the tremble in the adults.
So you stuffed
your own fear down
and became the calm.

The caretaker.

The one who didn't ask
for anything too heavy
because the house
already felt like it would tip over.

And that pattern?
It followed you.

You learned
to smile through heartbreak.
To organize the crisis.
To dry your own tears
before anyone could see them.

You made your needs smaller
so no one would feel
burdened by your pain.

You made your grief

convenient.
Digestible.
Brief.

And now?

No one checks on you.
Not really.

They assume you're okay.
They assume you'll figure it out.
They assume you're fine.

But you're not fine.

You're just **practiced.**

At hiding.
At functioning.
At bleeding
in ways no one
has to clean up.

Let me say it clearly:

You should not have had to earn
the right to collapse.

You should not have been forced
to choose
between being loved
and being vulnerable.

You are not weak
for being tired.

You are not broken
for needing rest.

You are not selfish
for wanting someone
to look at you and say:

"You don't have to hold it all anymore."

Fall.
If you need to.

Fall.

Into a softness
that doesn't ask you
to explain.

Into a silence
that doesn't punish you
for needing it.

Into a version of love
that isn't built
on your performance.

Let it crack.
Let it shake.
Let the mask
rot in the sun.

And when you're ready,

stand again.

Not because you have to.
But because you can.

Because the ground
is still here.
Because you
are not alone.

Because this time

you're not carrying
everyone else.

You're just carrying you.

And that is enough.

—The Sun

Letter 25: To the One Who Grew Up Too Early and Was Never Allowed to Return

You didn't get a childhood.
Not really.

Maybe you had toys.
Maybe you had birthdays
and backpacks
and report cards.

But you also had
secrets.

You had pressure.
You had silence
wrapped in responsibility.

You were the fixer.
The translator.
The peacekeeper.

**The emotional support adult
in a child's body.**

And no one noticed
they were stealing something sacred from you

your right
to just be.

So you grew up fast.

Learned how to read moods
before you knew how to spell your own name.

Became dependable.
Quiet.
Exceptional.

You made yourself useful
so you wouldn't be discarded.

You made yourself small
so no one would feel threatened.

But inside?

You were still just a kid.

One who wanted to be held.
To be protected.

To not know everything.
To not have to carry
everyone else's emotional mess
like it was your birthright.

And now?

You're grown.
But the grief is still there.

Because you never got to be soft.
You never got to be a mess.
You never got to be safe enough
to regress.

People admire your strength.
Your insight.
Your wisdom.

**But no one asks
what it cost you.**

No one sees the girl,
the boy,
the kid
who never got to

not know.

Who never got to just…

breathe.

So let me say this plainly:

84

It wasn't fair.
It wasn't okay.

You should not have had to become
the adult in the room
before your bones were done growing.

And no,
you're not too old to reclaim it.

You're not too far gone
to reach back.

You can still be soft.
You can still be silly.
You can still play.

You can still let someone else
carry the bag
for once.

You are allowed
to take off the armor.

You are allowed
to rest in arms
that don't need you to be strong first.

You are allowed
to cry about what you never got.

And if no one else says it?

I will:

I see the child in you.
She's still there.
He's still waiting.
They're still hoping.

Not for a second chance

but for someone to finally say:

"You shouldn't have had to do that alone."
"You shouldn't have had to grow up like that."
"You can come home now."

You can.

And when you do

I'll be right here.

—The Sun

Letter 26: To the One Who Always Has to Translate Themselves to Be Understood

You're fluent
in yourself.

But the world
doesn't speak your language.

So you code-switch.
You soften.
You trim your thoughts
into palatable shapes.

You swap metaphors
like currencies,
trying to explain what should never need defending:

your essence.

You say things
five different ways
just to be heard once.

You edit your face.
Your tone.
Your joy.
Your grief.

Because experience taught you
too much truth
makes people uncomfortable.

Too much you
makes people leave.

So now
you carry a **translator**
in your throat,

always buffering your realness
through layers of strategy
and self-monitoring.

You've become brilliant
at being legible.

But inside?
You ache
for someone to just get it.

To get you
without requiring
footnotes
or disclaimers.

And I need you to hear this:

That ache
is not too much.

**It's your soul
remembering what it means
to be seen
without effort.**

You were never meant
to live your whole life
in the margins
of someone else's understanding.

You were never meant to carry
the burden of being both

the poem
and
the translator.

You deserve a room
where you don't have to explain your metaphors.

Where your laughter
doesn't need context.

Where your silence
is read as depth,
not danger.

Where your full spectrum
isn't just tolerated
it's recognized as sacred.

Stop mistaking
exhaustion
for humility.

You are not hard to love.

You are hard to colonize.

And that
is a gift,
not a flaw.

So rest your translator.

Speak
in your mother tongue.

Let your sentences
come whole
and holy.

The ones
who are meant to hear you?

They will.

They always do.

—The Sun

Letter 27: To the One Who Thought They Were the Problem, But Were Just in the Wrong Room

You spent years
thinking it was you.

Too much.
Too intense.
Too sensitive.
Too loud.
Too deep.
Too needy.
Too… you.

So you shaved yourself down.
Edited your voice.
Softened your truths.

Made yourself easier to love.
Or so you hoped.

But it still didn't work.

You still didn't fit.
You still felt like a stranger
in your own skin.

They called you dramatic.
Said you were overthinking.
Told you to be grateful.
To be realistic.
To be less.

And maybe you believed them.
For a while.

Until you couldn't anymore.

Because something in you
refused to die.

Even after all the shrinking.
Something in you whispered:

90

**"What if I'm not the problem?
What if I've just never been met?"**

And here's the truth:

You weren't too much.
You were just in rooms
built for smaller truths.
Smaller hearts.
Smaller lives.

You kept trying to bloom
in soil that couldn't hold you.

That's not failure.
That's misplacement.

You are not a problem.
You are a revelation.

And not everyone is ready for that.

But that doesn't mean
you should hide.

**You are not meant to fit every room.
You are meant to find the ones
that expand around your presence
instead of flinching from it.**

You are not meant
to be watered down.

You are meant
to be witnessed.

So go where you are seen.

Not just admired.
Not just tolerated.

Seen.

Because the right room
will feel like a homecoming.

And you'll realize
you were never asking for too much.

You are just finally
with people
who could hold what you carry.

—The Sun

Letter 28: To the One Who Still Doesn't Know What They're Meant to Do

You keep waiting
for the lightning.

The sign.
The clear, undeniable calling
that tells you:
"Go here.
Be this.
This is your thing."

You've read the books.
Made the lists.
Tried the paths
that promised clarity.

And still

You're circling.
Uncertain.

Exhausted
from the weight of potential
with no direction.

You look around and think,
**"Everyone else seems to know what they're doing.
Why don't I?"**

But love

they don't.
Not the way you think.

Most people are improvising.
Most people are choosing
what's close,
what's safe,
what makes sense
to the people around them.

You?

You never wanted just a job.
You wanted to matter.
You wanted to feel lit up.
You wanted to belong
to yourself
even if it didn't make sense
on paper.

And that kind of life?

Doesn't arrive fully formed.

**It's revealed,
one gut-pull
at a time.**

So stop waiting
for the epiphany.

Start listening
to the small, holy hunches.

The random idea
that won't leave you alone.

The thing you do
when no one's watching.

The curiosity
that doesn't go away
even when you try
to talk yourself out of it.

You don't find your purpose.

You build it.

Through devotion.
Through experimentation.
Through a hundred quiet yeses
to things
that feel like you.

Let it be messy.
Let it take time.
Let it unfold.

But stop telling yourself the lie
that you're lost
just because you're still in motion.

Wanderers aren't failures.
They're seekers.

And seeking
is holy.

—The Sun

Letter 29: To the One Who Doesn't Know What They Believe Anymore

You used to know.
Or at least,
you thought you did.

There were answers.
Or rules.
Or something that felt
like a path.

Maybe it was religion.
Or politics.
Or a belief in hard work,
good timing,
karma,
God.

Maybe it was just the idea
that if you did things right
life would turn out okay.

But somewhere along the way,
the foundation cracked.

Maybe the system
failed you.

Maybe the prayers
went unanswered.

**Maybe the people
who were supposed to embody the truth
turned out to be
the biggest liars.**

And now?

You're floating.

Not an atheist.
Not a believer.

Not cynical.
Not inspired.

Just…

tired.

Tired of pretending
you're sure.

Tired of trying to explain
something
you don't even have language for anymore.

Tired of feeling
like you're the only one
wandering through the fog
without a lighthouse
to aim for.

You're not.

You are not alone
in this strange in-between.

This sacred unknowing.

This place
where the old maps
disintegrated

but the new ones
haven't been drawn yet.

You are not lost.

You are in the wilderness.

And the wilderness
is holy.

You don't need to rush
to a new conclusion.

You don't need to pick
a new label.

You don't need to have
a polished story
about what you believe now.

All you need
is presence.

And maybe

a willingness
to let your soul speak
before your certainty does.

You haven't failed.

You're evolving.

And that's allowed
to be messy.

Let it be.

—The Sun

Letter 30: To the One Who's Tired of Holding the Line

You've been
the stable one.

The dependable one.

The "rock."

People don't check on you
they lean on you.

And you let them.

Not because
you don't need anything.

But because
asking
feels like adding weight
to people
who are already drowning.

So you stay upright.

You stay functional.

You stay kind.

But inside,
you're tired.

Not just physically

existentially.

Tired of being
the container
for everyone else's storms
while yours
go unnamed.

Tired of holding it together
because you know what happens
when you don't.

Tired of being
the translation point
for people
who don't know how to feel.

You don't want applause.

You want relief.

You want
one place
just one
where you don't have to
narrate your pain
to make it palatable.

You've learned
to look "fine"
even while bleeding.

To explain your needs
in bullet points.

To cry quickly,
quietly,

and then apologize
for the inconvenience.

But you were never
meant to be a structure.

You are not a bridge.

You are not a scaffold.

**You are not
a landing pad
for other people's wreckage.**

100

You are a human.

With limits.

With softness.

With a soul
that is aching
for something other than
maintenance.

So here is your permission:

You don't have to keep
holding the line.

You can let go.

You can fall apart.

You can disappoint the people
who only loved you
for your steadiness.

Because your freedom
is not in proving
you can carry it.

It's in remembering

you were never supposed
to carry it
alone.

—The Sun

Letter 31: To the One Who's Always Preparing for the Other Shoe to Drop

You don't relax.

Not really.

Even in joy,
your shoulders
are tight.

Even in love,
your stomach
is bracing.

Even in rest,
your mind
is scanning for cracks
in the foundation.

You know how to be grateful
and terrified.

You know how to smile
and catastrophize.

You know how to build
a beautiful life
while secretly wondering
when it will all
fall apart.

It's not because you're ungrateful.
It's not because you're negative.

It's because you learned
early
**that good things
are fragile.**

That safety
is a story
people tell themselves

until the universe
decides otherwise.

So now you rehearse grief
before it arrives.

You feel
pre-loss.

Pre-disaster.

Pre-emptive pain
like some kind
of cruel insurance policy.

And you think
it makes you ready.

But all it really does
is rob you
of the sweetness
you were finally
starting to taste.

So let's name it.

The other shoe
might drop.

The phone
might ring.

The diagnosis
might come.

The goodbye
might be unexpected.

But that's always been true.

And if it's always true
then none of your bracing
is actually
protecting you.

It's just
stealing the joy
from the moments
that are real,
and warm,
and safe.

**You deserve to live
inside the good
while it's still good.**

You deserve
to trust the ground
under you
even if it isn't permanent.

Even if
it changes tomorrow.

Let yourself be soft.

Let yourself be still.

Let yourself
have
what you have.

Because this moment?

This now?

This ordinary beauty?

It doesn't need
to be earned.

It just needs
to be felt.

And no matter
what's coming

you'll face it
stronger

if you've allowed yourself
to feel joy
in the meantime.

—The Sun

Letter 32: To the One Who's Afraid Their Best Years Already Happened

You feel it
in your stomach
sometimes.

That creeping thought
you don't say out loud:

"What if it's all downhill from here?"

What if I missed it
my moment,
my magic,
my life?

You scroll past
younger faces,
braver voices,
people who still look
excited
when they talk about
the future.

And something in you
aches.

Not with jealousy
with grief.

Because you used to be
like that too.

Bright-eyed.
Full of
"one days."
Not yet tired.

Now you're tired.

And wise.
And wary.

And unsure
if any of it
is still possible.

You wonder
if you waited too long.

Or if you chose wrong.

Or if the door
has quietly closed
and you just
haven't accepted it yet.

But let me tell you
something true:

Your life
is not a peak.

It is a rhythm.

And your magic?

It is not
behind you.

It is
within you.

You are not late.
You are not over.
You are not done.

You are ripening.

And that's
a different kind
of beauty.

One with roots.
One with edge.
One that doesn't

beg
to be seen

because it knows.

You are not here
to recreate
your past self.

You are here
to meet
the version of you
that only
time
could grow.

So don't go numb.

Don't stop reaching.

Don't stop choosing
days
that still have
color in them.

You are not
a has-been.

You are a becoming.

Let your best years
hear you
coming.

—The Sun

Letter 33: To the One Who's Afraid They've Peaked Already

You had
a moment.

Maybe it was small.

Maybe
it was everything.

But for one
stretch of time

**you were lit
from the inside.**

Inspired.
Certain.
Alive.

You felt
chosen.

By love.
By art.
By purpose.

By something
that made you
want to stay.

And now?

Now you're wondering
**if that
was it.**

If that was the only time
you'll ever feel
that kind of fire.

If everything after
is just
echo.

You scroll
through old photos.

Reread
old journals.

Try to remember
who you were
before the spark
faded.

And part of you
is proud.

But part of you
is haunted.

Because no one told you
that joy
could feel
like a ghost.

That the high points
would hurt
on the way down.

That you'd keep
measuring now
against then

as if aliveness
has an expiration date.

Let me tell you
something.

You didn't peak.

You tasted.

You touched
the edge
of something true.

And now,
you know
what's possible.

That's not
a loss.

That's a compass.

So stop
trying to replicate
the exact moment.
The exact circumstances.
The exact you.

Because the next version?

It won't look the same.

It's not
supposed to.

It will be stranger.
Wider.
More yours.

There is life
after the highlight reel.

There is beauty
in the ordinary.

There is magic
that doesn't need
a spotlight
to prove it's real.

You didn't peak.

You just
got a glimpse.

Now go meet
the rest of it.

—The Sun

Letter 34: To the One Who's Afraid They Missed Their Moment

You keep replaying it.

That one decision.

That one relationship.

That one fork in the road
where you *could've* said yes,
should've gone left,
might've changed everything.

And now
you live with the ache of almost.

Of what could've been.

Of the version of your life
that might've existed
if only you'd been braver,
or faster,
or ready.

You see people younger than you
doing things you still dream about.

You see your peers settled into lives
you're not even sure you want
but the comparison still stings.
Still scrapes.
Still whispers:
"You're too late."

And some days?
You believe it.

You believe
the window closed.
You believe
the door won't open again.
You believe
your moment came and went
while you were blinking,

grieving,
working,
surviving.

But let me say this plainly:
You did not miss your life.

**You were just not ready for the one
that would *actually* belong to you.**

Not the performance.
Not the imitation.

Not the "almost enough"
version you would've settled for
just to quiet the fear.

Your real life
the one stitched with your name
requires presence.

And presence requires
readiness.
And readiness often comes
at the cost of delay.

So no. You didn't miss it.

You ripened.
You endured.

**You got strong enough
to stop running after
what wasn't real.**

And now?
You're not chasing a moment.

You're meeting it.

Eyes open.

Heart steady.

No apology.

Let the others sprint.
Let the clocks tick.

You are not too late.

You are right on time.

—The Sun

Letter 35: To the One Who Thinks We're All Being Dramatic

You roll your eyes.

You scroll past.

You hear people talk
about burnout,
loneliness,
existential ache

and all you can think is:
"Get over it."
"Work harder."
"Be grateful."
"Life's not that bad."

You don't mean to be cruel.

**You just
don't get it.**

You don't see the point
in picking at wounds
that never seem
to heal.

You think all this self-reflection
is just an excuse
to avoid responsibility.

To stay soft.
To stay stuck.

But here's what I see:

You've never had the luxury
of falling apart.

You've never been allowed to say,
"This hurts,"
without someone

telling you
to toughen up.

So, you stopped naming pain.

You stopped noticing
your own.

You built an identity
around "sucking it up"

and mistook it
for strength.

You think you're above it.

But really?

You're armored.

You think everyone else
is "too sensitive."

But the truth is:
you've just gone
numb.

And numbness?

Isn't strength.

**It's grief
in a straightjacket.**

You mock
what you don't understand.

Because you were never given
a safe place
to understand yourself.

You're fluent in silence.
In sarcasm.
In suppression.

But deep down,
some part of you knows:

You're tired, too.
You're lonely, too.

You've just been taught
to keep your ache
quiet
and your face
hard.

So let me say
what no one ever did:

You don't have to hold it
all alone.

You don't have to be
the strong one
forever.

**You don't have to dismiss
tenderness
to survive.**

This isn't about coddling.

It's about remembering
you're human.

And there's a difference
between resilience
and self-abandonment.

You're not
above the ache.

You're inside it.

And the moment
you stop performing
invincibility

118

that's the moment
you actually
begin to heal.

We're not being dramatic.

We're just not
pretending anymore.

And maybe,
you don't have to
either.

—The Sun

Intentionally left blank. Use for notes, if needed.

Part II: The Marriage of Ghosts

This is the graveyard of unspoken things.
Where love didn't collapse. It *faded*.
Not in flames.
But in drafts and silences.

The texts got shorter.
The eye contact less certain.
The jokes didn't land like they used to.
And still…you stayed.

This is where grief lives inside functioning relationships.
Where the grief doesn't scream.
It just *lingers*.
Like perfume from someone who's already left the room.

Some of these ghosts wear wedding rings.
Some still say "I love you."
Some sit across from you at dinner
and talk about the weather like it's intimacy.

Others vanished mid-conversation, mid-season, mid-life plan
but their absence still answers every question you never got to ask.

This section is for the griefs that don't get funerals.
The friendships that dissolved without ceremony.
The lovers who never truly arrived.
The family members who stayed in your life
but stopped seeing your face.

This is what it costs to keep pretending.
To keep performing connection.
To stay in rooms where your soul is starving,
just because leaving would make things *messy*.

These letters are hauntings.
You might recognize the ghost.

Letter 36: To the Couple Who Became Co-Parents But Forgot to Stay Lovers

You love each other.

You love your kids.

You love your life
most of the time.

You're a good team.

You handle the schedules.
You pass the baton.
You clean the spills,
answer the questions,
keep the house from burning down.

You're doing it.
You're making it work.

But somewhere along the way

you stopped seeing each other.

Stopped flirting.
Stopped playing.
Stopped reaching for each other
just because.

Stopped making eye contact
for longer than three seconds.

And you tell yourselves:
"It's just a phase."
"We're busy."
"We'll reconnect eventually."
"This is just what parenting looks like."

And maybe that's true.

But also?

You are more than parents.

And your love deserves to live
outside the checklist.

Because what happens
when the kids grow up?
When the house is quiet again?
When the to-do list
is suddenly empty?

Will you still know
how to reach for each other?

Will you even remember
who you were before
you became Mom and Dad?

Or will you be strangers
with good memories?

You don't need a date night.

You need desire.

You need presence.

You need to look at each other
not as co-managers of a household
but as two souls
still choosing one another.

Let the dishes sit.
Let the kids be bored.
Let yourself want them again.
Let yourself be wanted.

This is not about guilt.

It's about returning.

To the part of you
that once got nervous around them.

To the part of you
that still knows
their body,
their laugh,
their mind.

To the part of your love
that existed
before the calendar
ran your life.

You're not too far gone.

You're just overdue
for a moment
that isn't for anyone else
but you two.

Make one.

Soon.

—The Sun

Letter 37: To the Couple Who Are Still Together, But Not Really Here

You're still a team.

Still sharing space.
Still managing the life
you built together.

And from the outside?

You're solid.
You're functioning.
You're still "together."

But inside?

Something's shifted.

And neither of you
is saying it out loud.

It's not a war zone.
No betrayal.
No screaming fights.

Just quiet.

A silence that used to mean comfort
but now feels like distance.

You talk,
but only about the necessary things.

You touch,
but it's muscle memory.

You're not strangers.

But you're not really here, either.

You've both gotten so good
at adapting

that you didn't notice
when the connection began to fade.

But the truth is:

Love doesn't die in one big moment.

It drifts.
It recedes.
It forgets how to knock.

And you stop opening the door
because it feels easier to function
than to feel.

But neither of you
wants to live
in that kind of quiet grief.

Because you remember.

You remember
laughing.
You remember
staying up too late talking.
You remember
the thrill of being seen
really seen
by each other.

And you want that again.

Even if you don't know
how to ask for it.

So here's your invitation:

Don't wait for a breaking point.

Don't wait for someone
to cheat,
or cry,
or leave.

Name it now.

Name the quiet.
Name the space.
Name the part of you that
misses what you once were.

Not with blame.
Not with panic.

With presence.

Say:
"I still love you.
But I miss us."

"I want more than comfort
I want aliveness."

"Can we find each other again?"

This isn't about starting over.

It's about starting from here.

With eyes open.
With honesty.
With courage.

You're not too far gone.

You're just out of practice.

But love remembers.

And if you're both willing
you can still meet each other
at the door.

—The Sun

Letter 38: To the Man Who's Married But Secretly Lonely in His Own Home

You're not in crisis.
You're not yelling.

There's no affair.
No explosion.

You're just... fading.

You wake up.
You move through your day.
You text when you need to.
You watch a show together.
You sleep on your side.
You get up
and do it again.

From the outside?

You're doing fine.
Stable.
Responsible.
Still married.

But inside?

You feel like a ghost
in your own life.

You used to talk.

Not just about groceries
or bills
or the kids

talk.

With spark.
With curiosity.
With presence.

Now it's schedules.
Now it's
"Did you feed the dog?"
Now it's
"What time is your thing tomorrow?"
Now it's scrolling in silence
while the TV plays a show
neither of you really loves.

And you wonder:

"Is this just what marriage is?"
"Is this all there is?"

You love her.

You're not looking to leave.

But you're not sure
if either of you
is really there anymore.

You wonder
if she even sees you.

If you've both gotten so good
at functioning,
you forgot how to feel.

So let's name the thing:

You are lonely.

And loneliness
inside a relationship
is a different kind of grief.

Because you're not alone.

You're just unseen.

You're giving,
but not being met.

You're showing up,
but not being felt.

And no one would believe you
if you said it out loud
because everything looks
"fine."

But here's the thing:

**It doesn't have to end
to change.**

You don't have to blow it up.

You just have to get honest.

With yourself.
With her.
With the part of you
that's been sleeping
longer than your body has.

Ask the questions.

Not with blame.
Not with panic.
With presence.

"Do you still see me?"
"Do you miss us?"
"Are we even in love…still?"

Maybe she's feeling it too.
Maybe she's just as afraid
to say it.

**Maybe this moment
is your threshold.**

You're not broken.
You're not ungrateful.
You're just waking up.

And if you're brave enough
to speak what's true

this doesn't have to be
the slow fade into nothing.

**It can be the beginning
of something real.**

—The Sun

Letter 39: To the Woman Who Feels Like She's Disappearing Inside Her Own Marriage

You're still here.
Still waking up.
Still holding it down.

Still checking
the calendar,
remembering
the dentist appointment,
paying
the bill no one noticed
was overdue.

You're doing everything you promised.

**And somehow,
you're still vanishing.**

Not all at once.

Not dramatically.

Just...
little by little.

A slow erosion
of joy.
Of being wanted.
Of feeling like you're more
than a roommate
with shared logistics
and good manners.

There's no fight.
No obvious betrayal.
No big crisis.

Just that quiet ache
that no one talks about:

What if this is all it ever is?
What if I give my whole life to someone
who stopped looking at me
years ago?

You sit next to each other
on the couch,
but it feels like miles.

You try to talk,
but it's always about things,
not you.

You want to be touched
but not out of obligation.

And deep down,
you wonder:
"Is it me?"
"Did I get boring?"
"Am I asking for too much?"

No, love.

You're not asking for too much.

You're asking to be met.
To be felt.
To be held in a way that says:

"I still see you.
I still want you.
You're not just my partner
you're my person."

That's not a fairytale.
That's basic soul maintenance.

And if you're not getting that?

You're not broken for noticing.

You're awake.

You don't need to blow it up.

But you do need
to stop pretending.

Stop
smiling when it stings.
Stop
carrying both sides
of the emotional labor.
Stop
being so understanding
that you disappear
in your own kindness.

You are still here.

And you deserve
to be met—fully.

Not just as a wife.
Not just as a mother.
Not just as a capable woman.

As you.

So say the thing.

Even if your voice shakes.
Even if he gets defensive.
Even if it makes the air between you
colder
for a little while.

Say it:
"I miss us.
I miss me.
I want more."

Because you're not crazy.

You're just no longer willing
to go numb
inside a marriage

that forgot how to make room
for your soul.

Let this be the moment
you come back to life.

And if he can meet you there?

Rebuild.

And if he can't?

Then let this be the year
you finally choose you.

—The Sun

Letter 40: To the One Whose Partner Doesn't See Them Anymore

They don't mean to hurt you.
They're not cruel.
They don't scream
or cheat
or disappear.

They're just…
not looking.
Not really.

They pass you the remote.
They text when they'll be late.
They say "love you"
as they walk out the door.

They touch you
sometimes
but not like before.

And maybe they think everything's fine.
Maybe you even say it is.

But inside?
You're starving.

Not for drama.
Not for attention.

But for contact.

The kind that says:
I still see you.
I still feel you.
I still choose you.

But these days,
you're background.
You're assumed.
You're efficient.
You're fine.

And you start to wonder:
"Did I fade?
Or did they stop looking?"

You start to shrink your needs.
You start calling your longing too much.
You start excusing the distance

they're tired.
they're stressed.
this is just what coupling looks like.

But love without presence
isn't love.

It's performance.
It's muscle memory.
It's a house with no lights on.

**You deserve to be looked at
like you're still a wonder.**

You deserve to be touched
like you're still tender.
You deserve to be asked,
"Who are you now?"
and to be listened to
when you answer.

This isn't about blame.
It's about truth.

It's about naming the ache
before it hardens into resignation.

So say it.
Say, "I don't feel seen."
Say, "I want more than functioning."
Say, "I want to be felt,
not just tolerated."

And if they can meet you there
look again,

listen again,
love again

rebuild.

But if they can't?
If they keep loving you
in autopilot?

You don't have to disappear
inside their comfort.

You still deserve
a full-body yes.

And I promise
someone out there
is still looking.

So don't forget
how to be seen.

Start with yourself.

—The Sun

Letter 41: To the One Who Became Everything and Still Isn't Enough

You did it all.
You were what they needed.
What they asked for.
What they didn't even realize
they were demanding.

You shapeshifted.
You translated your heart
into their language.
You made yourself
efficient.
Helpful.
Low-maintenance.

You kept the peace.
You read between the lines.
You stayed three steps
ahead of disappointment.
You made it easy
to love you.

**And somehow,
they still didn't.**

At least not in the way
you were hoping.
Not in the way
that fills
instead of drains.
Not in the way
that stays.

And now you're exhausted.

Because you've spent a lifetime
becoming
and still,
it wasn't enough.

You learned the lie too young:
That love is something you earn.
That safety comes from control.
That being wanted
means being useful.

So you became everything.

And now you don't even know
what you are
without the performance.

Just a shell of strategies.
A catalog of pleasing behaviors.
A ghost in a costume
labeled "good."

But here's what they never told you:

**Becoming everything for someone else
is the fastest way
to lose yourself.**

It's not that you're too much.
It's that they asked too little
of themselves.

You never had to contort.
You never had to audition.
You were enough
before you did a damn thing.

So let this be the line you draw.

Let this be the moment
you stop chasing approval
like it's oxygen.

Let this be the season
where you reclaim your form.

Not as a role.
Not as a mirror.

Not as an answer
to someone else's wound.

But as your whole self.
Unrevised.
Unapologetic.
Un-pleased.

You are not here to be enough for them.
You are here to be real with you.

They'll either rise to meet you
or you'll finally be free enough
to leave.

—The Sun

Letter 42: To the One Who's Afraid They're Asking for Too Much

You've rehearsed it
in your head
a hundred times.

Softened the edges.
Made it sound casual.
Tried not to sound

needy,
dramatic,
or like a problem.

You don't even know
if what you're asking for
is big

or if you've just been taught
to shrink
so long

that anything honest
feels like a demand.

You want presence.

You want to be held
when you're quiet.

You want someone
to remember
what you said yesterday.

You want to feel

**like your joy
matters as much
as your labor.**

You want to be listened to
the first time
without a breakdown.

But still,
something in you whispers:

Don't ruin it.
Don't be difficult.
Don't need too much.

So you dial it back.
You pick your moments.

You tell yourself
to be grateful.

You tell yourself
they're trying.

You tell yourself
it's not that bad.

You tell yourself
to stop expecting so much.

But here's the truth:

You are not asking for too much.

You are remembering
what *enough* feels like.

You're not high maintenance.

You're emotionally fluent
in a world
that forgot
how to listen.

You're not needy.

You're just done
living on crumbs.

You're not dramatic.

You're just waking up
to your own hunger.

There is a war in you

between the part
that's still afraid
to be "too much,"

and the part
that knows what it is
to feel deeply unmet.

**Stop wounding yourself
to keep the peace.**

**Stop editing your needs
down to what won't scare people away.**

The right ones
won't be scared.

The right ones
will say thank you.

For telling the truth.
For giving them a chance to show up.
For choosing connection
over comfort.

Let this be
the last season
you make yourself small
in the name of survival.

You are not a burden.
You are not a test.
You are not too much.

You are a whole damn signal.

And the people
who are meant for you

will hear you
loud and clear.

—The Sun

Letter 43: To the One Who Misses Being Touched Without Earning It

You're not touch-starved.

You're
permission-starved.

Because touch
has become a reward,
not a right.

You've noticed it
haven't you?

The way affection
waits for good behavior.

The way your body
only gets reached for

when you're
easy,
pleasant,
or useful.

You're loved conditionally,
and the condition
is always:

don't need too much.

So now
you barter with yourself.

"Don't get upset
just be good."

"Don't bring it up
just wait until it passes."

"Don't make it weird
just stay wanted."

You've made yourself
smaller
just to be held.

And maybe
no one's said it outright

but your nervous system knows.

You've trained it
to equate stillness with safety,
compliance with closeness.

But here's the thing:

You're not meant to be held
only when you're
clean,
calm,
and convenient.

**You are not meant
to earn tenderness
like a treat
for doing tricks.**

You are not
a reward.

You are not
a break.

You are not
a job well done.

You are
a body.
A soul.
A being.

And you are
fucking starving.

This is not about sex.

This is about access

to warmth,
to presence,
to being wanted
when you're a mess.

It is a violence
to grow up believing

**that affection
must be traded
for obedience.**

You've internalized it
so well

that now
you police yourself.

But that ache in you?

It's not weakness.
It's not high maintenance.

It's the part of you that remembers:

you once received love
without having to audition for it.

Let that memory
burn through the lies.

You don't need
to be sweeter.
You don't need
to be easier.
You don't need
to be less.

You need
to be met.

On your worst days.
In your loudest hours.

Without having to perform
a single
goddamn
thing.

That's not a luxury.

That's
your birthright.

Stop settling for scraps.

—The Sun

Letter 44: To the One On The Receiving End Of Someone Else's Rage

You keep trying
to be the calm
in the storm.

But the storm
keeps moving
into your house.

And somehow,
**you're the one
mopping up after it.**

Maybe they told you
it was stress.

Or grief.

Or just how they
process things.

Maybe they said
they're just passionate.
That they didn't mean it
like that.
That you're too sensitive.

But here's what I want to say
as clearly as possible.

**Someone else's grief
is not a valid reason
to hurt you.**

Yes
they might be in pain.

Yes
they might be carrying
something heavy.

Yes
maybe their anger
has roots.

But you are
not the soil.

You are not
the punching bag
for someone else's healing.

This letter
is not about blame.

It's about
clarity.

Because over time,
you start
internalizing it:

their sharpness,
their moods,
their volatility.

You start shrinking
to avoid setting them off.

You start
doubting your tone,
your timing,
your truth.

You start thinking
maybe
you're the problem.

You're not.

What's happening is this:

**You've become the
landing zone**

**for someone else's
unprocessed grief.**

And while that might
explain
their behavior

it doesn't
excuse
it.

You are allowed
to love someone
and still say:

I will not absorb this for you.

You are allowed
to set the boundary.

To step back.

To say:
your pain is valid

but your behavior is not.

You don't owe
your peace

just to make someone else
comfortable
in their chaos.

You are not cruel
for protecting
your nervous system.

You are not selfish
for refusing to bleed

just because
someone else
is hurting.

152

This is your
permission slip.

To walk away.

To call it what it is.

To name the damage
that gets done
in the name of grief.

You didn't cause it.

And you don't
have to carry it.

—The Sun

Letter 45: To the One Who Realized the Fairy Tale Is Propaganda

You don't talk about it much.

But something cracked.

Quietly.

One day,
you just…
stopped believing.

Not in love

but in
the story.

The one they fed you
since you were small.

The one with the prince
(or princess),
the rescue,
the happily ever after

that never once accounted for
your **rage**
or your **rent.**

You used to reach for it
like a roadmap.

Now
it feels like a trick.

You're not bitter.

You're awake.

You saw behind the curtain
realized the castle
was a mortgage,

the gown
was unpaid labor,
and the romance came
with silence

about who you were
allowed to be
to stay wanted.

It hit you:

This whole thing was designed
to keep you chasing a promise
that kept changing shape.

Be desirable.
But not needy.

Be successful.
But not threatening.

Be independent.
But not so much
that no one gets to save you.

It was never about love.

It was about obedience.

And now?

Now you're standing
in the rubble
of a myth
that kept you small.

And you're asking:

What do I build instead?

That's the grief
of awakening.

The death of a dream
you didn't even realize
wasn't yours.

But here's the truth:

Love is still real.

But it might not look
like the story.

It might look like
rebuilding trust
in yourself.

Like finding joy
that doesn't need permission.

Like rewriting the ending
without waiting
for a co-star.

You don't need a fairytale.

You need a life
that doesn't

require disappearing

to feel chosen.

So grieve the dream.

Then go build
the thing
that doesn't lie to you.

—The Sun

Letter 46: To the One Still Bleeding from a Relationship They Pretend to Be Over

You say you're fine.

You even believe it
most days.

You're functioning.
You're smiling in pictures.
You're dating.
You're sleeping.
You're laughing
at the right moments.

And yet

There it is.

The flinch
when their name gets mentioned.

The way your body stiffens
at a scent,
a song,
a street.

The inbox
you check twice.

The silence
you can't quite unclench from.

You told yourself you let go.

You made it logical.
You walked away.
You said what needed saying.
You closed the loop.

**But closure is a myth
when the wound
is still wet.**

Because the truth is

You're still bleeding.

Still aching in places
no one can see.

Still walking through your days
like someone left
the window open

in the dead of winter.

And maybe the worst part?

You don't feel like
you have a right
to miss them.

Not anymore.

Too much time has passed.
Too many people have told you
to move on.
Too many smiles
you've faked through it.

But that ache
doesn't care about time.

That ghost
doesn't check the calendar.

It just lingers.

It just waits for you
to stop pretending.

So stop.

Stop pretending
you're not still holding
pieces of them.

Stop pretending
it didn't matter.

Stop pretending
you're over it

when your soul knows better.

This is not weakness.

This is memory.

This is love,
still echoing.

Let it echo.

Let it sting.

Let it mean something.

Because that's how it leaves.

Not by force.
Not by denial.
But by truth.

You're still healing.

That doesn't make you pathetic.

That makes you
human.

And when it's ready
to loosen its grip

it will.

But not before
you stop lying to yourself.

You loved them.

It mattered.

And even now,

it's okay
that it still does.

You're not behind.

You're just honest.

And honesty?

That's how we make room
for something real.

—The Sun

Letter 47: To the One Who Got the Apology They Waited Years For…And It Didn't Fix a Damn Thing

You thought
it would feel different.

You waited.

You hoped.

You rehearsed it
in your mind

what they might say,
how it would sound,
what you'd finally feel
when it came.

And then one day

they said it.

"I'm sorry."
"I shouldn't have done that."
"You didn't deserve it."

And for a second,

**you almost believed
this was the moment
everything would shift.**

That your chest would loosen.

That the fog would lift.

That some ancient knot
inside you
would finally untie.

But it didn't.

Because an apology
can name the hurt

but it can't undo the cost.

It can't return the years.

It can't unshape
the ways you learned
to survive.

It can't love you
retroactively

through all the lonely nights
you needed something
that never came.

You're not ungrateful.

You're just honest.

And honesty says:

they may mean it now

**but the damage
already happened.**

You still had to become
someone else
to live with the silence.

They said
"I'm sorry"

but they're not the one
who had to rebuild trust
from scratch.

They're not the one
who learned
to flinch at kindness.

They're not the one
who lost a piece
of their innocence

and had to keep going
like nothing happened.

So no

you're not cold.

You're not petty.

You're not
"holding onto the past."

You're grieving the life
you could've had

if someone had seen you
sooner.

Let yourself grieve that.

Not because you want
to stay in it

but because pretending
you're healed
just to make them feel better

**is another form
of betrayal.**

You're allowed to say:

"Thank you
for saying that."

And also:

"It still hurts."

You're allowed to mean both.

And you're allowed
to stop waiting

for their words
to fill the hole.

They won't.

But you can.

With your own voice.
With your own boundaries.

With the small,
steady practice

**of not needing
the people who hurt you
to be the ones
who heal you.**

It didn't fix it.

But maybe
it frees you.

Not because
they finally saw

but because now,
you finally can.

—The Sun

Letter 48: To the Ones Who Don't Know If They Were Ever Really Loved

You replay it sometimes,
don't you?

That one moment
the laugh,
the look,
the hand
that almost stayed.

You wonder if that was it.

If that was
the proof.

But it's slippery,
isn't it?

Love
that needs
to be decoded.

Affection that only arrived
dressed as obligation,
or strategy,
or control.

You tell yourself
not to be dramatic.

You list all the times
they showed up.

You inventory the birthdays,
the gestures,
the groceries bought,
the texts returned.

You build a case
for love
like it's on trial.

But still

**something in you
doubts the verdict.**

Because what
you were really asking
was:

Did they cherish me?
Did they see me?
Did they stay
when I stopped performing?
Did they hold me
when I broke?

Or did they
just like the version
of me
that smiled through it?

It's okay
not to know.

It's okay to admit

that you needed more
than what they gave.

It's okay
to stop digging
through the rubble

looking for a diamond
that was never there.

Sometimes
the ache isn't about
what you lost.

It's about what was
never offered
honestly.

But here's
the revolution:

**You get to stop
waiting for retroactive love.**

You get to stop
translating absence
into affection.

You get to name
the void

without apologizing
for it.

And then
you get to fill it.

With truth.

With people
who meet you
without barter.

With love
that doesn't
make you beg.

You were always worthy
of the kind of love
that didn't leave you guessing.

And you still are.

—The Sun

Letter 49: To the One Who Knew They Were a Placeholder and Stayed Anyway

You knew.

Maybe not right away.

But eventually
you felt it.

That subtle
hollowness
in their kiss.

That delay
before they texted back.

That ache
you swallowed
every time
they looked past you

while talking
about their future.

They liked you.

They cared,
even.

But you were the
"for now"
not the "forever."

**And something in you
clocked it
long before the words
ever made it
to the air.**

But you stayed.

You adjusted.

You turned down
your hunger
and called it
patience.

You made yourself
convenient,
pleasurable,
undemanding.

You wore compatibility
like armor,

hoping it would
become chemistry.

Because maybe
just maybe
if you loved them enough,

they'd see it.

See you.

Want you.

Choose you.

But they didn't.

And deep down,
you always knew
they wouldn't.

So let's name it:

This is grief.

Not just
for what didn't happen

but for what
you did to yourself

trying to keep
their maybe alive.

You didn't just
lose them.

You lost
the parts of you
that tried to shrink

into their almost.

That's what hurts,
isn't it?

That you saw
the writing on the wall

and tried
to learn the language

instead of
walking away.

But hear me clearly:

You are not stupid.

You are not weak.

**You are not some
desperate fool
who mistook crumbs
for dinner.**

You are someone
who wanted to be loved
so badly,

you tried to make
a temporary space
feel like home.

There's no shame
in that.

But there is cost.

And now
you're the one
who has to pay it.

So let yourself feel it.

The waste.
The regret.
The anger at yourself

for not leaving
the first time
you knew.

But then
forgive yourself.

Not because
it didn't matter.

But because
you do.

This is your invitation
to stop

being the backup plan
in your own life.

To stop auditioning
for roles

that don't require
your whole self.

You are not
a benchwarmer

for someone else's
someday.

You are not
a temporary stand-in

for a life
they haven't earned.

**You are the goddamn
main character.**

And it's time
you started
acting like it.

—The Sun

Letter 50: To the One Who Misses the Group Chat That Died Quietly

No one said goodbye.

No grand falling out
(or maybe there was).

Just fewer replies.
Longer silences.

A meme left on read.

A plan
that never got scheduled.

And slowly
like fog lifting

the thing you thought
would last forever

was just... gone.

**And it's embarrassing,
isn't it?**

To grieve
a group chat.

To miss
a digital thread

like it was
a lifeline.

To scroll back
through old messages

like you're flipping
through an old yearbook

from a version of yourself
that felt more alive.

But it *was* a lifeline.

During breakups.
During pandemics.

During jobs
that drained you

and mornings
that broke you.

They were there.

Not always in person
but present.

You had a place
to belong.

A circle
that got your jokes.

A thread
that felt like home.

And now?

Your phone's still there,

but the feeling isn't.

And no one talks about it.

Because how do you explain

that the silence
of a group chat

can feel
like a **death**?

But that's what it is.

A soft death.

**The kind that doesn't
earn a funeral**

**but still takes
something with it
when it goes.**

So let's name it:

You miss being known
in real time.

You miss being folded
into someone's day

without having
to earn it.

You miss the shorthand,
the emojis,

the stupid gifs
that made you snort-laugh

in line at the store.

You miss being seen

not just when
something big happened

but on an average Tuesday,

just because
you existed.

And you're not silly
for that.

You're not over-attached,
or nostalgic,

or "too sensitive."

You're just human.

**And humans are wired
for connection**

that lives
in the little things.

So here's your permission:

Grieve it.

That thread.
Those people.
That version of you.

It mattered.

And it doesn't make you weak

to notice the absence
of something

that used to feel
like presence.

But also
let yourself be available

to what wants
to take root next.

Not a replica.
Not a rebound thread.

Something new.

Because the truth is:

you didn't outgrow
connection.

You just outlived
a context.

And there are still people
right now

waiting for someone like you

to drop in,
crack a joke,
send a meme,
say:

"I'm here."

So go ahead.

Be the one
who starts
the next thread.

Even if no one responds
right away.

Even if it doesn't become
a new home.

Start it anyway.

**Because you know
what it meant**

**when someone
did that for you.**

—The Sun

Letter 51: To the One Grieving a Best Friend Who Didn't Die, Just Disappeared

You still don't
understand it.

You replay
the last messages

in your head
like an investigator

at a crime scene

searching
for the moment
it turned.

But there was
no betrayal.

No blowout.

Just space.

That strange,
stretching silence

where there
used to be
presence.

And you keep asking:

Was it me?
Did I miss a sign?
Did I hold on too tightly?
Did I not hold on enough?

**But sometimes
grief doesn't come
with clarity.**

Sometimes,
the person who knew
everything about you

becomes the ghost
who still walks
your memories.

You see something funny
and think,

I have to send this to

Oh.
Right.

You lost a person
and no one
brought you flowers.

You lost a language
that only the two
of you spoke.

You lost the witness
to entire chapters
of your life

and people act like
it's no big deal

because no one died.

But **something did die.**

The version of you
that only existed
in their company.

The comfort
of being known
without explaining.

The shorthand.
The inside jokes.

The simple miracle of:
I get you.

And now you walk
through your life

carrying a friendship
that's still technically alive

but unreachable.

A phone number
in your contacts

you scroll past
like a tombstone.

So let's name
the ache.

Let's stop pretending
it's not real

just because
they're not dead.

Let's stop shrinking it
because people think
only romantic breakups count.

You loved them.

Maybe still do.

And that love
doesn't vanish

just because
the texts stopped.

You get to grieve.

180

Even without closure.
Even without certainty.

Even if they're out there
laughing with new friends
who don't know your name.

**Because love that real
leaves echoes.**

And when those echoes fade,

you feel it
in your bones.

But also
you survived it.

You didn't shatter.

You kept showing up
for your life

with a heart
that still had
an empty chair
at the table.

That's not weakness.

That's sacred strength.

So here's to the friendship
that shaped you.

Here's to the one
who held your secrets,

laughed
till they cried,

called you
at midnight,

and disappeared
without a map.

And here's to
the version of you

who still knows
how to love

even after
loss without explanation.

You're not foolish
for missing them.

You're just human.

And humans remember.

—The Sun

Letter 52: To the One Who Always Texts First and Finally Stopped

You were always
the one who reached out.

The check-in.
The *"just thinking of you."*

The initiator.
The planner.

The one who made sure
the thread didn't unravel.

You didn't mind
at first.

You told yourself:
"That's just who I am."

You believed it meant
you cared more,

or were more available,

or just better
at connection.

**But it started
to sting.**

The hours
that turned into days.

The *"so sorry, just saw this"*
messages

that felt more like brush-offs
than replies.

The plans you suggested
that were met with
vague maybes.

The birthdays you remembered
that no one else
seemed to.

You told yourself
it was fine.

They're busy.
Everyone's busy.

But underneath
the rationalizing,

a small,
sharp truth
began to form:

**If I stop showing up…
will anyone notice I'm gone?**

So one day,
you did.

You didn't text first.
You waited.

And the silence
grew loud.

No one checked.
No one noticed.

Or if they did,
they didn't say anything.

And it gutted you
more than you expected.

Not because
you wanted attention

but because
you wanted to matter.

To be missed.
To be chosen
without prompting.

To feel like someone
would carry the thread
for once,

just to keep you close.

This isn't petty.

This is grief.

The grief of realizing
how much of
your connection
was one-sided.

The grief of admitting
that maybe,
it mattered more to you
than to them.

You're not crazy
for noticing
who doesn't reach out.

You're not needy
for wanting reciprocity.

You're not wrong
for wanting to feel wanted.

This is what
boundaries feel like
at first.

Lonely.
Exposing.

Like you've cut off
your own oxygen.

But you haven't.

You've just stopped
feeding something

that never fed you back.

And now comes
the space.

The silence.

The chance
to let new energy in.

People who text first.
People who remember.
People who choose you
without prompting.

You didn't stop texting first
to be cruel.

You did it because
you were finally ready
to see what was real.

And now you know.

Let the silence speak.
Let it reveal.

And let yourself
feel the ache

of how long
you held the thread
alone.

You're not hard to love.

You were just holding on
to people

who didn't know
how to hold you back.

You can stop now.

And something softer
can start.

—The Sun

Letter 53: To the One Who Couldn't Keep Pretending It Was Still Fun

At first,
it was real.

The laughter.
The inside jokes.

The nights that ran
long
and messy
and golden.

You meant it
when you said,
"God, I needed this."

But somewhere
along the way,
it started
to shift.

The group chat
turned into a performance.

The hangouts
felt more like obligations
than oxygen.

You laughed,
but it didn't land
in your body.

You smiled,
but it took effort.

You showed up,
but you weren't
really
there.

Still,
you kept going.

Because what kind of person
walks away
from the people
who've been there?

What kind of adult says,
"I don't want this anymore,"
when nothing
technically
went wrong?

You told yourself:
"Maybe I'm just tired."
"Maybe it's just a phase."
"Maybe I should be grateful."

But the truth?

You were done pretending.

**Done performing a version of yourself
that no longer felt alive.**

Done contorting your energy
into shapes
that kept the peace

but cost
your presence.

Because fun
real fun

doesn't leave you
feeling drained.

Real connection
doesn't require a script.

And joy?
Joy doesn't ask you

to betray yourself
just to be included.

So you let it fade.

Quietly.
Without explanation.

Not because you're cruel
but because something in you
finally whispered:

I don't want to feel this way anymore.

And that's not selfish.

That's sacred.

You honored the version of you
that was still alive
underneath the mask.

So if you're sitting
with the silence now

if you're wondering
whether you made it all up,
whether you quit too soon,
whether you're allowed to feel this much
over something
so ordinary

Yes.

Yes, you're allowed.
Yes, it was real.

And yes,
it's okay to grieve
something that quietly
stopped being good.

Some endings
don't explode.

190

They just…

finish.

You get to move on.

Without guilt.
Without guilt.
Without guilt.

—The Sun

Letter 54: To the One Who Shares DNA But Nothing Else Anymore

Blood
is not
enough.

You've been told it should be.

That family means forever.
That DNA is a tether
you can't undo.

That shared holidays,
old photos,
and childhood bedrooms
are reasons to stay.

But here you are.

Trying to grieve someone
who isn't dead
just unreachable.
Just different.
Just
not
safe
to keep inviting
into the soft places
of your life.

Maybe it's a sibling
who turned into a stranger.

Maybe it's a parent
whose love always came
with conditions.

Maybe it's a cousin,
an aunt,
a grandparent

someone who helped shape you,
but refuses to see
who you've become.

It's quiet grief.

Unacknowledged grief.

The kind people don't let you have
because "they're still alive,"

as if being alive
and being good for you
are the same thing.

But the truth is:

Some ties unravel.

Some family members
stay fixed in versions of you
that no longer fit.

Some people call it loyalty
when what they really mean
is silence.

You've tried.

Tried to explain,
to reconnect,
to extend grace.

Tried to hold your tongue
at Thanksgiving.

Tried to stay small
to keep the peace.

Tried to laugh off
the things that still sting.

But pretending
costs too much now.

It costs your dignity.
Your peace.
Your sense of safety
in your own story.

And maybe
you still love them.

That's the worst part,
isn't it?

Love that won't die
but also
won't save you.

Love that keeps flickering
but can't light the way
forward.

So here's the permission
you were never given:

**You do not owe anyone access
to your becoming.**

Not to those
who weaponize your past.

Not to those
who shrink you for sport.

Not to those
who think blood
absolves everything.

You can love them
and still choose distance.

You can pray for them
and still block their number.

You can wish them well
and still protect
your joy.

194

Family isn't
who shares your DNA.

It's who sees your soul
and stays.

You didn't fail.

You just stopped pretending
that proximity is connection.

That biology
is belonging.

And that clarity?

That's not cold.

That's
freedom.

—The Sun

Letter 55: To the One Who Knows They'll Never Be Fully Understood by Their Family

You're not making it up.

You've tried
God, have you tried.

You toned it down.
You softened the edges.

You used
smaller words,
polite silences,
nervous laughter.

You played the role.
Sat at the table.
Smiled through the static.

You kept hoping maybe
this time
they'd ask the real question.

The one that reaches you.

Not your job.
Not your relationship.
Not your latest accomplishment.

But you.

It never comes.

They love you
sure.

In the way
they know how.

But that love
wraps around a version of you
they've decided is

acceptable.
Palatable.
Predictable.

And anything outside of that?

Feels like a threat.
Or worse
like nonsense.

So you edit yourself
into something
smaller.

You leave parts of your story out.
You swallow
the weird,
the wild,
the sacred,
the broken.

Because every time
you showed them
your full self

You saw the flicker
in their eyes.

The way the conversation shifted.
The way you became
the awkward one.
The difficult one.
The drama.

And eventually,
you learned:

It's easier not to say anything at all.

But easier
doesn't mean
it doesn't hurt.

Because there's a grief
to being loved
in approximation.

To having people
who are technically "there,"
but never truly
with you.

You could win a Nobel Prize
or sob your way
through a breakdown,

and they'd respond
with the same blank phone call:

"Okay, well... did you eat?"

They're not monsters.

They're just unequipped.

But that doesn't make the loneliness less real.

And I need you to hear this:

You are not too much.
You are not ungrateful.
You are not broken
for wanting to be met.

You are just
awake.

Awake in a lineage
that has survived
by going numb.

Awake in a family
that may never
be able to mirror you back.

But you
do not have to disappear
to belong.

And you
do not have to amputate
the truest parts of yourself
just to keep the peace
at Thanksgiving.

Their understanding
is not
your oxygen.

You are allowed
to stop reaching
for their permission
to be whole.

You are allowed
to create
chosen family
that doesn't just "put up with you"
but gets you.

You are not the black sheep.

You are the first light.

And while they may never
fully see you

you are still here.
Still real.
Still radiant.

No translation required.

—The Sun

Letter 56: To the One Carrying the Weight of Being the Responsible Sibling

You didn't choose this role.

You just got good at it.

While the others
spiraled,
wandered,
rebelled

you steadied.

You became
the reliable one.
The planner.
The fixer.

The one who knew
when the bills were due,
what medications were needed,
how to keep the family
from falling apart.

You were praised for it.

"Thank God for you."
"You're the glue."
"You're the strong one."

And you smiled through it.

Because what else could you do?

No one asked
if it was fair.
If you were tired.
If you ever wanted to be the one
who fell apart a little.

If you longed
to be held

instead of holding
everyone else.

Your reliability
became a trap.

Your competence
your cage.

Because the more you showed up,
the less they believed
you needed anything
in return.

And maybe
you believed it too.

That being loved
meant being useful.
That love is earned
through endurance.
That your needs
are an afterthought
to everyone else's chaos.

But let's tell the truth.

You are not infinite.

You are not
the family's emotional dam.

You are not selfish
for wanting out of a role
you never auditioned for.

You are allowed to rest.
To ask for help.
To not answer every text.

To say:
"I can't fix this."
To say:
"This is not mine to carry anymore."

Being the responsible one
doesn't make you
more evolved.

It makes you
exhausted.

And under that exhaustion?

There's grief.

Grief
for the childhood
you didn't get to fully live.

Grief
for the moments
you had to grow up too soon.

Grief
for the way
your strength became
a requirement
instead of a gift.

So here it is,
plain and sharp:

You don't owe anyone your depletion.

You're not disloyal
for wanting your life back.

Being the stable one
doesn't mean
sacrificing your soul.

You can still be loving
without being
everyone's life raft.

Let someone else
take a turn.

Let the chaos
find its own legs.

You're allowed
to be whole
without being responsible
for holding
the whole family
together.

—The Sun

Letter 57: To the One Who Never Thought They'd Still Be Alone

You told yourself
it would happen.

Eventually.

A partner.
A family.
A life shared.

You believed it.

Maybe even
built your life around it.

But the years passed.
The holidays got quieter.
The text threads dried up.

And now?

**You're looking around
wondering if you're
the last one standing.**

You didn't plan for this.

You didn't choose
to be alone.

You're not anti-relationship.
You're not "too picky."

You're just…
still waiting.
Still hoping.
Still trying
not to let the ache
eat you alive.

And people try to help

They tell you
to love yourself.
To enjoy your freedom.
To stop looking
and it'll happen.

But they don't understand

what it means
to go to sleep
every night
with no one
to tell the small stories to.

What it means
to move through illness,
success,
heartbreak,
with no one
who's just yours
to bear witness.

What it means
to be the third,
the extra,
the afterthought

when everyone else
is a unit.

So let's tell the truth:

It hurts.
It's lonely.

And it feels like
some cosmic oversight
that you
of all people
are still waiting
for a hand to hold.

But here's what's also true:

Your life is not on pause.
You are not missing.
You are not unfinished.

You are
a whole world.

And anyone who joins you
is not completing you
they are witnessing you.

Your solitude
is not a punishment.

It's a season.
It's a refinement.

It's an honoring
of the depth you carry
and the love
you're still worthy of.

There is no shame in longing.
No shame in wanting more.

But don't forget:

You are still someone's dream.

You are still magic.
You are still here.

And it is not too late.

Not for love.
Not for partnership.
Not for the life
that still has your name on it.

—The Sun

Letter 58: To the One Who Feels Like They're Always a Step Outside Belonging

You're invited
but only after
the plans are already made.

Included
but only in a way
that feels polite.

Tolerated.
Not chosen.

You show up,
you try,
you smile
when it stings.

And then you go home
and wonder
if you're imagining it.

If maybe
you're just sensitive.

If maybe
they like you enough
and that should be enough.

But it never is,
is it?

**Because some part of you
still feels
like you're knocking on a door
that never fully opens.**

You know how to adapt.
You always have.

You mirror.
You manage.

You shrink
the parts of yourself
that feel "too much"
or "too different."

And still
you leave the room
feeling
a little bit invisible.

Here's the truth
you haven't been told:

It's not you.
It's the shape the world insists you contort into.

It's the culture
of cool detachment,
the subtle exclusions,
the unspoken codes
no one taught you
but punish you
for not knowing.

You are not imagining it.

There is a cost
to being the one
who feels deeply,
asks real questions,
wants actual connection.

And the world
doesn't always reward that.

But don't confuse
being unchosen
with being unworthy.

Don't mistake
social friction
for personal failure.

You are not outside
because you're wrong.

You're outside
because you're real.

And being real
in a world
that rewards masks
is a kind of exile.

But even exile
can be sacred.

Because somewhere

there are others
who don't want performance either.
Who are done pretending.
Who will meet you at depth.
Who will see you

not as decoration,
but as revelation.

Hold your shape.

Don't dilute yourself to belong.

**The ones who are meant to find you
will recognize you
exactly as you are.**

And when they do?

It will feel like breath returning.

—The Sun

Letter 59: To the One Scared They'll Die Alone

You don't say it out loud.

You keep it tucked
beneath your strength,
beneath the jokes,
beneath the calendar
full of plans.

But there are nights
when the silence
is louder than usual.

When the door doesn't open,
the phone doesn't ring,
and the ache creeps in:

What if it never happens for me?

What if the love you want
never arrives
in the form you've been taught to expect?

What if no one picks you?

What if you are
the last one left
carrying the weight of a future
that keeps not coming?

And worse

**what if it means something
about you?**

That you're too much.
Or not enough.
That you missed your window.
That you made
too many wrong turns,
and now it's too late
to be found.

But here's the unspoken truth:

**This fear isn't just about love.
It's about vanishing.**

About the unbearable thought
that no one
might witness the whole of you
and still choose to stay.

But you?

You are not a consolation prize.
You are not the sum
of your coupledness.
You are not behind.

You are a whole life.

Not half of one
waiting to be completed.

Love may come.

And if it does,
let it meet you
not as someone desperate to be filled
but as someone
who already claimed themselves.

And if it doesn't come
in the form they promised
the hand in yours,
the shared last name,
the joint checking account

that does not mean
you were unloved.

**Some souls
are monuments.**

Too big
to be fully held
by another.

But never unseen.

So keep living.

Big.
Messy.
Honest.

Fill your rooms
with music.

Eat the beautiful food.

Make the memories
that will haunt the walls
long after you're gone.

You do not need a witness
to prove you were worth watching.

But just in case
no one's told you

I see you.
And I'm not looking away.

—The Sun

Letter 60: To the One Parenting Without Backup and Pretending It's Fine

You don't have the luxury
of unraveling.

There's no one coming.
No one picking up the slack.
No one tagging in
so you can lie on the floor
and sob into a towel.

There's just
you.

And the child.

And the clock
that doesn't stop.

So you do it.

You wake up
when you're dead tired.
You make food
you don't want to eat.
You answer questions
you don't have the energy
to answer.

You hug
when you're touch-starved.

You carry the weight of the world
in your body,
and no one calls it a miracle.

**They just call it
your job.**

And maybe
you're "technically" not alone.

Maybe there's an ex
who shows up
sometimes.

Maybe there's a parent
who offers advice
but not presence.

Maybe there's a partner
in the house
who's checked out
in everything
but name.

But functionally?

You are it.

The system.
The source.
The safety net.
The calendar.
The backbone.
The everything.

And it's not that you don't love your kid.

You do.

You'd die for them.
You have died,
in small ways.

Over and over.

Dreams deferred.
Bodies run ragged.
Loneliness swallowed
so they never see the ache
in your eyes.

But still.
You ache.

214

And the worst part?

You feel like you're not allowed
to say any of it
out loud.

You're afraid people will hear you
and think:
"You chose this."
"You should've known."
"You're lucky to even have a child."

So you carry it
quietly.

You laugh at the memes.
You post the smiling photos.
You show up
with the lunch packed,
the homework signed,
the soul
threadbare.

But I see you.

**You are parenting through
the kind of exhaustion
that steals names
from your mouth.**

You are holding a world together
with one hand
and picking Cheerios out of the couch
with the other.

You are the definition of grace under pressure
but grace doesn't mean
you're okay.

So let this be your **permission**.

To cry in the shower.
To leave the dishes.

To tell someone,
"I'm not fine."

To stop performing invincibility
and just fucking break
if only for a moment.

You are not weak.
You are not failing.

You are doing the impossible
in a world
that expects it to look easy.

And you deserve backup.

Even if it's just someone saying:
"I see you.
I get it.
You shouldn't have to do this alone."

Let this be that.

Let this be your moment
of being held.

—The Sun

Letter 61: To the One Who Thought Parenthood Would Be Different

You love your child.

That's never been the problem.

But this isn't what you pictured.

Not the exhaustion.
Not the erasure.
Not the constant negotiation
between who you are
and who you're supposed to be
now.

You thought
there'd be more joy.

More connection.
More moments that made the sacrifices
worth it.

Instead,

**there are days
you feel like a machine**

dispensing snacks,
rules,
reminders,
and rides.

You're not ungrateful.

You're just tired
of being reduced
to utility.

No one warned you
about this kind of grief

The grief of becoming
a parent
and slowly disappearing.

The grief of losing
the freedom
to even think
a full thought.

The grief of loving
someone more than life itself
and still sometimes wishing
you could run.

They don't tell you
that sometimes
parenthood feels like a trap.

That you'll miss your old life
so much it aches.

That your identity
will fracture,
then disappear,
then rebuild into something
no one prepared you for.

And when you try to name it
this ache,
this loss,
this internal scream
people say,
"But you chose this."

**As if that disqualifies
your pain.**

As if choosing love
means you forfeited
your humanity.

**Here's what I'll say instead:
You're not broken.
You're not a bad parent.**

You're just waking up
in a role
that asked for everything
and rarely gives you back
the parts of yourself
it consumed.

But you still matter.

Not just as "Mom"
or "Dad"
or "the one who holds it all together."

You.

The whole,
wild,
complicated soul
inside the tired body.

So let this be your reminder:

You're allowed
to grieve the version of parenthood
you didn't get.

You're allowed
to need things
big things.

And you're allowed to say,
"This isn't what I imagined.
But I'm still here.
And I'm still me."

**You're not failing.
You're just learning how to exist
inside a love
that sometimes forgets
to leave you room.**

—The Sun

Intentionally left blank. Use for notes, if needed.

Part III: The Quiet Thirst

This is the part of you that still *wants*.
Even after the silence.
Even after the betrayal.
Even after you promised yourself you were done needing anything at all.

It's the flicker you can't smother.
The ache that hums beneath the numbness.
The quiet thirst for softness, beauty, *more*
even when hope feels like a setup.

You don't call it desire.
You barely admit it exists.
But it's there.
In the way you linger at open doors.
In the way your body remembers music it hasn't heard in years.
In the way you ache when someone looks at you like you *matter*.

This section is not about collapse.
It's about aftermath.
The slow, maddening hunger that follows survival.
The part of you that dares to whisper:
What if I still get to want something better?

These are not promises.
They are thresholds.
They won't feed you.
But they'll remind you you're still starving.

And that?
Is something like life.

Letter 62: To the One Who Can't Find Meaning Anymore

You've tried.

God, you've tried.

You've read the books.
Made the lists.
Said the affirmations.
Done the work.
Kept the routine.
Showed up like someone
who believes the story they're in.

But lately?
It all feels... blank.

Muted.

Like the subtitles are on
but you can't hear the sound.

**You're not in crisis
but you're not alive either.**

You're floating.
You're functioning.
You're faking warmth
you can't feel.

And people would never guess.

Because you're still doing the things
answering emails,
picking up groceries,
saying "I'm good!"
with just the right tone.

You're still posting.
Still laughing.
Still being grateful.

But under all of it?
You're wondering:

Is this all there is?

Not because you're ungrateful.
Not because you're dramatic.

But because something real in you
is starving.

And the life you're living
no longer feeds it.

The danger isn't that you'll give up.
It's that you'll stay in the numbness so long
you'll forget you were ever hungry.

So here it is,
plain and sharp:

Meaning doesn't always arrive
with fireworks.

Sometimes it starts as
discontent.
As a refusal.
As the quiet knowing:

this
isn't
it.

You don't have to know
what "it" is
yet.

You just have to stop pretending
you don't feel
the void.

This isn't about quitting your job,
or leaving your relationship,

or booking a flight
to somewhere dramatic.

It's about telling the truth.

About what you crave.

About what's gone quiet.

About what no longer
makes you feel like
you.

**You're not broken.
You're bored of the lie.**

And when the lie stops working
that's when the real story begins.

Start small.

Pick up the book
that doesn't make sense yet.

Ask the question
no one wants to answer.

Follow the flicker,
not the map.

It won't make sense yet.
That's okay.

You're not building a brand.

You're recovering
your soul.

And meaning?

It's not waiting for you
in some perfect plan.

It's buried underneath
the life you stopped feeling inside.
Go dig.

—The Sun

Letter 63: To the One Who Gave Up Dreaming and Doesn't Know How to Start Again

You used to dream.

Not the big, flashy kind
they make movies about

but the quiet,
soft-edged kind.

The kind that lived in your chest
and whispered,
"maybe…
just maybe…
that could be me."

But somewhere along the way,
you stopped listening.

Not because you stopped wanting.
**But because life
made it too damn expensive.**

They told you
to be practical.
To choose the stable thing.
To be grateful
for what you have.

And you tried.

You did the right things.
You built the life.
You checked the boxes.

You survived things
you don't even talk about anymore.

And now?

There's space.
A pause.

226

A quiet
you weren't prepared for.

And in that quiet...
you feel how long it's been
since something lit you up
from the inside.

But the dreams?

They're distant now.
Fuzzy.
Like trying to remember
someone's face
you haven't seen in years.

And you don't know
how to find your way back.

So let me say this plainly:

You are not too old.
You are not too late.

You are not foolish
for wanting more.

Dreaming is not childish.

It's sacred.

It's the soul
refusing to die quietly.

But dreaming again
after loss?
After disappointment?
After proving
you can live without it?

That takes bravery.

So start small.
Start secret.

Start with the thing
that feels ridiculous
and tender
and entirely yours.

Start without needing it
to be "successful."
Start before you believe
you deserve it.

Make a list
of things you used to love.
Make a playlist
that feels like you at sixteen.
Buy the journal
you'll probably forget to write in.

Go stand
in the aisle of possibility
even if you walk out
with nothing.

The point isn't the dream itself.

It's the re-opening.
The risk of wanting again.

Because when you give yourself
permission to want
even quietly,
even clumsily

you come back
to life.

You're not done.

The world hasn't even met
the version of you

that stopped surviving
and started listening
to the part of you

that still believes
in something more.

Go meet them.

—The Sun

Letter 64: To the One Who Wants to Start Over But Doesn't Know Where to Begin

You're not broken.

But something in you
is done.

You're not in crisis
but the life you built
feels like a costume now.

You go through the motions,
but every day
tastes like copy paper.

You keep asking
the same question
in silence:

"Is this really it?"

You did
what you were supposed to do.
You got the job.
You showed up.
You kept the peace.
You played the part.

And now
you're standing
in the house
you built with your bare hands,
quietly wondering
why you feel like a ghost
inside of it.

No one talks about this part.

How success
can be suffocating.
How comfort
can feel like a coffin.

How something can look "fine"
and still feel
like a funeral.

And so you think
about starting over.

But the weight of it
freezes you.

You think:
"But I can't walk away from this."
"But I've invested too much."
"But people are counting on me."
"But what if I ruin everything?"

So you stay.
Half-alive.

Making micro-adjustments.
Convincing yourself
that numbness
is better than risk.

But here's the truth
no one gave you:

You don't need to know exactly where you're going.
You just need to stop lying about where you are.

You don't need
a five-year plan.
You don't need
a rebrand.
You don't need
a grand story.

You need
one brave breath.
One honest sentence.
One refusal
to keep sleepwalking.

You are not too late.
You are not too old.
You are not ungrateful for wanting more.

You are just waking up
in a world
that taught you
to be proud
of your cage.

Start with the truth.

Say it out loud
even if it scares you.
Especially if it scares you.

This isn't a collapse.

It's a returning.

You're not starting over.

You're starting true.

And the moment
you say what's real
your life starts meeting you there.

—The Sun

Letter 65: To the One Who Outgrew the Life That Once Fit Them

It used to feel right.
Maybe even
beautiful.

The job,
the city,
the people,
the rhythm of your days

It all made sense
once.

You chose it
for a reason.
It held you.
It shaped you.
It got you through.

But now?

It's too small.

Like trying to breathe
inside a room
with no windows.

Like wearing a coat
that used to warm you
but now just reminds you
how cold you are.

You're not ungrateful.
You're just awake.

And what you're waking up to
is the quiet truth
that life can't stay the same
when you're
no longer the same.

You've stretched.
Softened.
Shed things.
Seen too much
to pretend now.

You try to make it work.
Try to love it
like you used to.

But every time
you force a smile
or say "I'm fine,"
something in you
winces.

Because you know.

You've changed.

**And pretending not to
is killing you quietly.**

Here's what no one tells you:
Outgrowing something
doesn't mean it was wrong.

It means
you've grown.

And that's not failure.
That's proof
of life.

You don't owe
your past self
an apology
for becoming someone new.

But I know it's scary.

To walk away.
To say
"this isn't me anymore."

234

To step into the unknown
when the known
still feels safer
even if it's
suffocating.

**But staying in a life
that no longer fits
is its own kind of grief.**

You deserve a life
that matches your expansion.
You deserve
to feel
your full wingspan.

Not just
the safe, folded version.

So if it feels too tight
if it feels
like you're disappearing

that's your soul
telling you:

We've gone
as far
as we can go here.

You don't have to
blow it up tomorrow.

But you do have to
listen.

Start
with one honest sentence.

To yourself.
To someone you trust.

Say it:

"This isn't it anymore."

And let that truth
be the first
crack of light
in a brand new sky.

You're not done.

You're just beginning again.

—The Sun

Letter 66: To the One Who Wonders If It's Too Late

You look around
and whisper the question
no one ever answers honestly:

"Did I miss my chance?"

You try not to ask it.
You try to stay grateful.
You try to focus on the good

because yes,
there is good.

But still…
something aches.

You wonder
if the window closed
while you were being responsible,
or surviving,
or putting others first.

You wonder
if you gave your best energy
to a life
that wasn't even really yours.

You scroll past people
who are younger,
faster,
louder.

You watch them "arrive"
while you're still circling the block,
trying to remember
where you put your map.

And that cruel voice comes back:
"You waited too long."
"You should've done this years ago."
"It's too late now."

But here's the truth, love:
It's only too late if you believe
the clock is God.

And it isn't.

There is no divine stopwatch.
No sacred schedule you've ruined.
No expiration date
on becoming real.

There's just you.
And the part of you
that never stopped wanting.

That part is still alive.
Still kicking
under the weight of all your silence.
Still hoping
you'll come back for it.

And you can.

You can still fall in love
with your life.
You can still surprise yourself.
You can still bloom
fully
without apology.

You are not behind.
You are not a failure.

You are not
too old
or too tired
or too broken.

You are right here.

Which means
it's not too late.

Which means
it still matters.

Which means
you
still
matter.

The world hasn't seen
all of you yet.

But it will.

If you're brave enough
to begin again
even now.
Especially now.

—The Sun

Letter 67: To the One Who's Aching for a Soft Place to Land

You're so good
at holding it together.

At catching your own fall.
At stitching your life back up
quietly,
cleanly,
with no witnesses.

No one sees
the bruises forming
under the smile.

No one hears
the sound your soul makes
when the door closes behind you
at night.

You are the strong one.
The one who always figures it out.
The one who knows
how to keep moving.

But just because
you can do it alone
doesn't mean
you should have to.

You've learned
to wear resilience like armor.
To dress up depletion
as independence.
To call your exhaustion
"being capable."

And it's killing something tender inside you.

You need rest.

Not just sleep
but the kind of rest
that comes from being met.

The kind
that doesn't ask you
to perform first.

The kind that says:
"Come in anyway.
You're safe here."

You deserve a landing place
that doesn't feel like a test.

You deserve a relationship
where softness isn't punished.

You deserve a love
that doesn't mistake your silence
for strength.

I know how hard it is to admit it.

To say:
I'm not okay.

To whisper:
I want to be taken care of.

To let someone see
the ache you've wrapped
in competence.

But it's okay to need.
It's okay to not be the strong one for once.

It's okay
to want a place to crumble
without being asked
to explain yourself.

You are not a burden.
You are not too much.

You are not weak
for longing to be held.

And when that soft place
finally finds you

don't flinch.
Don't run.
Don't talk yourself out of it.

Let yourself land.

—The Sun

Letter 68: To the One Who's Starving for Beauty But Can't Justify the Time

You miss her.

The version of you who
used to sit in the sunlight,
or get lost in a book,
or wander into art museums
just to feel something.

You used to notice things.

Colors.
Textures.

The way the wind moved
through a curtain.
The way music curled
around your spine.

But now?
Beauty feels like a luxury.

A guilty pleasure.
Something that has to earn its place
between errands
and emails.

You scroll instead.
You swipe instead.
You keep going
because stopping feels indulgent.

Because somewhere along the way,
you learned that beauty doesn't count
unless it's productive.

But let me tell you what you already know:
You are starving.

Not for food.
Not for sleep.
Not for love, even.

But for beauty.

The kind that doesn't explain itself.
The kind that doesn't ask permission.
The kind that doesn't do a damn thing
except remind you
that being alive can still feel good.

You are not here to be efficient.
You are not a machine.
You are not a spreadsheet
of goals and tasks
and bills and groceries.

You are a body.
You are a soul.
You are a sensor,
made to feel.

And when you deny yourself beauty
you shrink.
You lose color.
You go grayscale.

So this is your permission slip.
Not to escape
but to return.

To your senses.
To wonder.
To whatever it is
that reminds you
you're more than what you produce.

Paint badly.
Buy flowers for no reason.
Light the candle.
Walk slower.
Touch the fabric.
Play the song again.

Let it be pointless.
Let it be sacred.
Let it be yours.

You do not need to earn it.
You only need to let it in.

—The Sun

Letter 69: To the One Who Can't Remember the Last Time They Felt Magic

You used to feel it.

Didn't you?

Not the wands-and-wings kind
but the breathless, weightless kind.

The kind that made you forget time.
The kind that cracked
something open in your chest
and let the light in.

The kind that made you feel
like maybe, just maybe,
life was on your side.

But somewhere along the way,
you traded it.

For schedules.
For certainty.
For being reasonable.
For holding everything together
like a person who doesn't need wonder to survive.

And maybe you don't.
But surviving isn't the point.

You didn't come here
just to get through it.
You came here to feel it.

But no one told you
magic would cost so much.

That it would ask you to slow down.
To believe in things without evidence.
To risk looking foolish

or dramatic
or too sensitive.

So you got quiet.
You got efficient.
You got productive.

You called that growing up.

But growing up was never meant to be a burial.
Especially not for your aliveness.

So let's say it plainly:

You are not wrong for wanting awe.
You are not weak for craving beauty.

You are not broken
just because nothing feels like enough anymore.

You are not too old for wonder.
You are too starved for it.

And you don't need a life overhaul.
You just need a crack in the shell.

One tiny act of devotion to joy.
One candle lit with no reason.
One song played too loud.
One moment
where you let your heart show
without apologizing for it.

Magic isn't gone.
It's just waiting
for you to look up.

You don't have to believe in miracles.
You just have to notice
when the air changes.

You were never meant
to harden into a task list.

You were meant to be moved.

So let it move you.

—The Sun

Letter 70: To the One Who's Ashamed of Their Own Longing

You keep it quiet.

That soft,
searing ache inside you.

You call it
"too much."
You call it
"childish."
You call it
"unrealistic."

But it's not.

It's your soul
trying to speak through the static.

You've been taught to shrink it.
To edit yourself down
to what's acceptable.
To want just enough to function
but never so much
that it threatens anyone's comfort.

So you act chill.
You act grateful.
You act like your deepest wants
are silly luxuries.

You say:
"It's fine. I don't need that. I'm good."

But you're not good.
You're starving.

And worse
you feel guilty
for the hunger.

You think you should

be over it by now.
You think you should
be more grateful.

You think longing is proof of failure.

But longing isn't weakness.
It's clarity.

It's your body
remembering something
your mind has tried to forget:

You were made
for more than coping.

Your ache is holy.

Your desire is not a flaw to fix.

It's a compass.
It's the map.

And yeah
wanting things you don't have yet
hurts.

But burying the want?
That's a different kind of death.

So no more shame.
No more pretending you don't care.
No more swallowing yourself whole
to be more digestible to the world.

Let the longing speak.
Let it sting.
Let it shape you.

You don't have to apologize
for wanting beauty,
softness,
belonging,

wildness,
magic.

You don't have to earn
your right to feel that pull.

You just have to
stop abandoning it.

You were born to want.
And you were born
worthy
of what you want.

Say it out loud.
Even if your voice shakes.
Especially if your voice shakes.

**The hunger is not the problem.
It's the path.**

—The Sun

Letter 71: To the One Who Feels Like It Shouldn't Be This Hard to Live

You wake up
already tired.

Not just in your body
in your bones.

In the part of you that remembers
when life still felt like something to be lived,
not just gotten through.

And the truth is:
You're not asking for much.

You're not chasing luxury,
fame,
excess.

You just want enough.

Enough energy
to move through a day
without crashing.

Enough money
to not panic
at the grocery store.

Enough time
to feel something
before collapsing into sleep again.

Enough space
to not feel like you're drowning
inside your own life.

But adulthood wasn't supposed to feel like this.

A never-ending treadmill
of bills,

expectations,
and quietly breaking.

The smile you wear at work
is a mask.

The jokes you tell your friends
are shields.

And under it all,
you're quietly whispering:

"Why is this so fucking hard?"

You wonder if it's just you.
If maybe you're too sensitive.
Too dramatic.
Too ungrateful.

**But it's not you.
It's the world.**

It's the system
that sold you a lie
and then blamed you
for not thriving inside it.

You were told
that adulthood meant freedom.

But nobody mentioned the invisible chains

The mental math
at every gas pump.

The guilt
when you rest.

The pressure to be productive
even in your grief.

The way survival became your baseline
and anything above that
feels like asking for too much.

You're not weak.
You're aware.

You see the absurdity
of a world
where people burn out
just trying to stay afloat.

You feel the weight
of holding up a life
that's built more for labor
than living.

And let me say this
as clearly as I can:

You are not broken.

You are breaking
under something
that was never meant
to hold you.

So pause.

Let yourself feel
how not okay this is.

Cry if you need to.
Scream if it helps.

But do not gaslight
your soul
into silence.

Because your pain
is not personal failure.

It is proof
of your aliveness
in a world that numbs.

It is resistance.

It is evidence
that your spirit still knows
what's sacred.

Still believes
that joy is not a luxury
but a right.

You are not asking for too much.

You are asking
for a life
that makes sense.

And that means
you are still whole enough
to imagine something better.

Hold onto that.

—The Sun

Letter 72: To the One Who Doesn't Know Who They Are Without the Struggle

You've always had something
to fight.

A crisis.
A deadline.
A person.
A system.
A version of yourself.

You learned how to armor up
early.

To stay alert.
To be ready.
To always have a plan,
a retort,
a way out.

You made survival
look like stability.

But lately?

There's no war.
Nothing urgent.

Just silence.

And it's fucking terrifying.

Because without the noise,
the pressure,
the constant call to defend or produce

you don't know who you are.

You feel soft.
Exposed.

Unworthy of rest
you've earned
a hundred times over.

And that's the grief
no one talks about:

When you're so used to surviving,
peace feels like death.
Stillness feels like failure.

But hear me:

**You were not born
to only be useful in chaos**.

You are not only lovable
when you're bleeding.

You can be known
outside of pain.

You can be wanted
without needing to prove why.

There is a version of you

not flattened,
not medicated,
not numbed

who belongs
in **joy**.

Not because you earned it.
But because it is your inheritance.

You don't have to keep breaking
just to feel alive.

Let this be the moment
you stop trying to justify your softness.

Let this be the season
you learn how to exist
without an emergency.

You are allowed
to live.

Not just endure.

—The Sun

Letter 73: To the One Who Knows How to Hold Everyone, But Doesn't Know Where to Put Their Own Pain

You're the steady one.

The one they call
when it's falling apart.

The one who knows
how to listen,
how to soothe,
how to make the chaos
feel less sharp.

You've mastered the art
of showing up.

Of being calm
when others are cracking.

Of nodding with empathy
even when you're screaming
on the inside.

And they thank you.
They lean on you.
They praise your strength.

But no one ever asks
where you go
to fall apart.

Because you don't.

You fold it up.
You tuck it away.

You turn your grief
into usefulness.

It's not that you don't feel.
You feel too much.

But you've learned
that your pain
makes people uncomfortable.

So you make it smaller.
Or you hide it in productivity.
Or you tell yourself
it's not as bad
as someone else's.

You don't cry
in front of them.

You don't text the paragraph.

You don't say,
"I need you,"
because you don't know
what you'd do
if they didn't show up.

So you carry it.

All of it.

And some days,
it feels like you might break
from the weight.

But here's the thing:

You don't have to earn
your right to be held.

**You are not only lovable
when you're useful.**

You are not only worthy
when you're composed.

You get to have needs.
You get to be messy.
You get to be human.

And yes
maybe not everyone in your life
can hold you the way
you hold them.

But that doesn't mean
no one can.

It means you need
different rooms.
Different people.
Different mirrors.

Ones who don't flinch
when your hands are shaking.
Ones who don't need you
to translate your ache
into something pretty.

Your pain deserves
a place to land, too.

Not just the cleaned-up version.
Not just the captioned insight.

The real thing.

Let someone hold you.
Let it be ugly.
Let it be true.

You don't need to be the strong one
all the time.

You just need to be real.

And let yourself be met there.

—The Sun

Letter 74: To the One Who Thinks They're Hard to Love

You assume they'll leave.

That's the first thing.

Before anyone even shows up
you're already bracing
for the exit.

Not because you're dramatic.
Not because you're broken.

But because somewhere
back there,
you learned
love comes with conditions.

So you scan every room
for proof.

That your laugh
is too loud.
That your silence
is too much.
That your need
is a burden.
That your softness
is inconvenient.
That your scars
make you unworthy.

You don't believe
you're unlovable.

Not exactly.

**You just quietly believe
you're hard to stay with.**

Hard to choose.
Hard to keep choosing
when things aren't shiny

or easy
or new.

So you make it easier
for them.

You explain your triggers
in a cute list.
You keep your voice calm
when you want to scream.
You give them space
before they ask for it.

You tell yourself:
If I'm low maintenance,
maybe I'll be loved longer.

And when someone
finally leaves?

You don't even cry.
You just nod
like it makes sense.
Like of course
they'd go.

You saw it coming.
You always
see it coming.

But here's the truth
you've never said out loud:

You don't want someone
to tolerate you.

**You want someone
who adores you.**

Who reaches for you.

Who delights in your weirdness
and holds your ache
with reverence.

You want to be chosen
not out of obligation
or convenience
but with joy.
With clarity.
With want.

And you deserve that.

Not after you heal more.
Not when you become easier.
Not once you earn it.
Not twenty
(or thirty)
pounds lighter.

Now.
As you are.

You're not hard to love.

You've just been loving people
who never learned
how to stay.

—The Sun

Letter 75: To the One Who Feels Like a Supporting Character in Their Own Life

You show up.
You smile.
You do what needs
to be done.

You are reliable.
Predictable.
Necessary.

And still
somewhere in the background
of your own story,
you've started to wonder:

**"When do I
get to matter?"**

You're the helper.
The fixer.
The one who remembers birthdays
and keeps everyone
on track.

The one people count on
but rarely
ask about.

You're always there.
But rarely centered.

You watch other people
chase their dreams,
burn down their lives,
declare their truths,
take up space.

And part of you
cheers for them.

But another part?
It aches.

Because you were taught
that wanting too much
made you selfish.

That standing in the spotlight
was arrogant.

That your job
was to support
not shine.

So you made yourself small.
You made yourself useful.
You made yourself safe.

And now?
You're tired.

Of being backstage
in a life
you're supposed to be starring in.

Of shrinking your voice
to fit someone else's plotline.

Of being everyone's "rock"
while no one notices
you're crumbling.

So let's tell the truth:

**You are not
a side character.**

You are not
a plot device
for someone else's development.

You are not here
to facilitate
everyone else's becoming.

You are the whole
damn story.

You are the reason
the sun rises
in your world.

You are allowed
to want more
than being thanked
in the credits.

Start small
if you must.

Choose one thing
today
that's just for you.

Reclaim five minutes
of your own attention.

Say no
without a reason.

Say yes
without guilt.

This is not
a rebellion.

It's a remembering.

**You are not selfish
for wanting to feel
like the main character
in your own life.**

You are sacred.
You are central.
You are seen.

—The Sun

Letter 76: To the One Who Secretly Feels Behind...At Everything

You don't say it out loud.
You wouldn't dare.

But deep down,
it hums like background noise:

"I should be further
by now."

Further in your career.
Further in love.
Further in healing, maybe.

Or parenting.
Or money.
Or self-trust.
Or stability.

You smile.
You nod.
You cheer for others.

But some part of you
is always counting

Measuring.
Comparing.
Failing.

And the voice in your head
is so convincing:

Look at them.
Look what they've built.
Look how clear they are.
Look how late you are.

**But that voice
never tells the truth.**

It doesn't mention
the detours you survived.

The invisible labor
you carried.

The grief
you had no language for.

The battles
you fought
just to stay here.

It doesn't account
for the fact
that you're not just building a life

you're rebuilding
from all the things
that tried to end you.

You are not behind.

You are becoming.

And no timeline
can measure
what that really takes.

Maybe
you weren't meant
to arrive fast.

Maybe
you were meant
to arrive whole.

Let them run.
Let them shout
from their rooftops.

Let them post
their announcements
and milestones.

And let yourself
breathe.

You are not late.

You are deep.

And depth
takes time.

You are allowed
to unfold
in your own season.

And when you do?

It will not be small.

It will be right
on time.

—The Sun

Letter 77: To the One Who Was Told They're Not Beautiful

You don't forget.
Not really.

Not the first time you heard it said
out loud

or worse:
implied through omission,
silence,
dismissal.

The way they chose your friend
and not you.

The way someone said
you were "smart"
with just enough pause
to mean
but not pretty.

The way you were always
the wingman,
the afterthought,
the emotional support pet
for someone deemed
more desirable.

You learned to internalize it early:

Beauty was a hierarchy.

You weren't on it.

And that meant
you were going to have to earn everything.

Love would not be given
you'd have to compensate for your lack.

With humor.
With over functioning.

With being less picky.
With being grateful
for crumbs.

And even if you tried to fight it

tried the makeup,
the weight loss,
the styling,
the posing

you always knew:

**The system wasn't designed
to recognize you
as beautiful.**

It was designed
to make you chase it.

Forever
just out of reach.

Let's tell the truth now.

Beauty has never been
neutral.

It is a weaponized
social metric.

It is propaganda
wrapped in perfume
and Photoshop.

It is the gatekeeping spell
for who gets:

protected,
prioritized,
believed,
wanted.

And the real scam?

They made beauty
the entry fee
for tenderness.

As if only the conventionally desirable
deserve soft love.

As if only those
who match a colonial,
patriarchal,
algorithm-approved standard

are worthy
of being chosen publicly
and loved
fully.

It isn't just about vanity.

It's about survival.

Because if you're deemed
not beautiful

**the world treats your needs
as optional.**

Your grief
as dramatic.

Your dreams
as unrealistic.

This isn't just a heartbreak.

It's a spiritual theft.

But I came
to return
what was stolen.

Because none of this
is about you.

It never was.

It's about control.

About keeping people
trapped in self-doubt

so they spend their whole lives
trying to earn
what they were born
worthy of.

It's about the lie
that beauty is a limited resource

when the truth is,
it erupts from you
when you're most
alive.

You were never
not beautiful.

You were just never seen
by people who knew
how to look.

And here's the secret
they don't want you to know:

You get to stop
performing.

You get to define beauty
on your own terms

or walk away from it
altogether.

You get to say:

**My body is not a billboard
for desirability politics.**

You get to stop apologizing for

your face,
your skin,
your belly,
your joy,
your fucking
radiance.

Let this be the last day
you dull your light
to soothe
the eyes
of the blind.

You are beauty.

You are rebellion.

You are the spell-breaker.

**You are the goddamn
standard.**

With all the fire
they tried to extinguish,

—The Sun

Intentionally left blank. Use for notes, if needed.

Part IV: The Undoing

No one warns you:
grief doesn't just come for what you lost.
It comes for who you *used* to be.
For the masks that hardened into skin.
For the story you kept telling yourself just to survive.

This part of the book isn't about healing.
It's about unraveling.

The moment the lie becomes too heavy to hold.
The moment you look at the life you built, and realize it's killing you.
The moment you stop mid-sentence, mid-smile, mid-performance and think:
I'm done.

This is where the pretending ends.
Where the roles collapse.
Where you disappear, on purpose.

This is not noble.
It's not poetic.
It's not clean.

It's a reckoning.

And the choice is quiet but final:
Come back different.
Or don't come back at all.

This is The Undoing.
There is no softer way through.

Letter 78: To the One Sitting in the Rubble After the Illusion Shattered

You didn't just lose
a relationship.

Or a job.

Or a dream.

You lost the illusion
that it was ever
what you needed.

That's the part
no one talks about

how grief doesn't just come
for what we loved,

but for what we hoped
it could become.

You're not just mourning
what ended.

**You're mourning the version
of yourself
who believed
it could last.**

It's dizzying,
isn't it?

To look around
and realize
the scaffolding
was made of smoke.

To see the house
you built
in someone else's blueprint,

crumbled
in your hands.

Believing wasn't foolish.

It was brave.

It meant
you still had
hope.

You're not weak
for collapsing.

You're not broken
for being stunned.

This is what it means
to wake up.

It's okay
if you feel foolish.

Or furious.

It's okay
if you want to pick
through the wreckage
just to prove
it had to be real.

It's okay
if you miss the lie

it kept you warm,
even if it kept you
small.

But here,
in the silence,
something honest
begins.

Not perfect.

Not polished.

But yours.

And no one gets to tell you
how long
you can sit here.

In the quiet.

In the ache.

In the ruin
that made space
for your becoming.

Because when you rise

and you will

You'll build something
that doesn't disappear
when you finally
tell the truth.

With love,
The Sun

Letter 79: To the One Who Still Wants To Believe, But Can't Go Back

You still remember
how it felt.

To believe in something
so fully
it wrapped around your ribs.

To speak the words
without flinching.

To feel
chosen.
Protected.
Certain.

It was real
to you.

Maybe still is,
in the way
an old melody
lingers in your body
long after
the instrument
has been put away.

And you miss it.

Not because it was all true.

But because
it gave you something
to lean against.

A story
to stand inside.

A reason.

But now?

There's a crack.

And no matter
how gently
you try to step over it

it spreads.

Maybe it was something
someone said.

Maybe it was
the silence
in a moment
when you needed truth
and got script.

Maybe it was
watching someone suffer
while everyone else smiled
and said
this is part of the plan.

Whatever it was

you can't unknow
what you now know.

You still want to believe.

But not like that.

Not at the cost
of your integrity.

**Not by shrinking
to fit a story
that no longer fits you.**

This is the quiet grief.

Of reverence
tangled with betrayal.

Of love
that doesn't know
where to land
anymore.

And it's okay
to be here.

You don't need
to burn it all down.

You don't need
to pretend
it never mattered.

You're allowed
to hold
both the comfort
it gave you

and the pain
it caused you

in the same hand.

This isn't backsliding.

It's becoming.

You're not faithless.

You're just being honest.

And that, too,
is sacred.

—The Sun

Letter 80: To the One Who Realized What They Believed Was A Lie

You didn't mean
to build your life
on sand.

You were told
it was stone.

You were told
it was truth.

You were told,
this is the way it is.

And so
you believed.

Because believing
made you belong.

Because doubting
felt dangerous.

Because questioning
meant risking the story
that gave you safety.

But now
the edges don't hold.

The words don't land.

The rituals feel
hollow.

**The people
who once felt like home
now speak a language
you can't answer
without flinching.**

And that's grief.

The grief of realizing
you were shaped
by a story
that never fit

or worse,
never cared
for your becoming.

The grief
of having to unlearn
what you once defended.

The grief
of watching something crumble
that you once
would have fought
to protect.

It's disorienting.

Because when a belief breaks,
it's not just a thought
that shifts

it's an identity
that dissolves.

You're not
who you were.

You're not yet
who you'll become.

You're just standing
in the in-between,
with nothing in your hands
but honesty.

**And that
is everything.**

Let the story fall.

Let the silence stretch.

Let yourself mourn
what felt real
even if it wasn't.

You don't need
to rush
to the new belief.

You don't need
to reattach
to certainty.

You just need
to be here,

awake,

even if it hurts.

This is not failure.

This is freedom,
in its first
and most terrifying form.

And you
are not lost.

You're just
between truths.

—The Sun

Letter 81: To The One Who Fucked Around And Found Out

You knew.

On some level
you knew.

You flirted with the edge
like it couldn't cut you.

Played with lives
like they were rubber bands
that'd always
snap back.

And maybe they did.

Until the day
they didn't.

This grief?

This isn't about loss.

It's about cost.

The cost of thinking
you were the exception.

The cost of believing
I didn't mean to
was enough.

The cost of mistaking
attention for affection,

loyalty for forgiveness,

silence for approval.

Maybe you thought
the rules didn't apply to you.

Maybe you were hurting
and wanted someone else
to hurt too.

Maybe you were just scared,

and stupid,

and sloppy
with people
who deserved better.

Whatever the story…**you found out.**

And now you're here,
standing in the fallout,

sifting through the broken glass
of a mirror
you shattered
with your own hands.

This is not
a letter of absolution.

But it *is*
a letter of recognition.

Because there's a particular kind of grief
that lives inside regret.

It howls
in hindsight.

It aches
in the quiet
of no one calling you back.

It walks beside you
every time
you replay
what you could've done
differently.

And if you're honest
really honest

this might be the first time
you've ever felt
your own weight.

So feel it.

Don't turn away.

Don't spiritualize it.

Don't blame
your childhood,
your ex,
or the full moon.

Just stand there.

Let it burn.

Let it scar.

Let it mean
something.

Because if this grief
teaches you
how to be someone
worth trusting

then maybe, just maybe

you didn't fuck up
for nothing.

—The Sun

Letter 82: To the One Who Realized They're Part of the Problem

It hit you sideways.

Not in the middle of a fight,
not in the fallout,
but in the quiet after

when no one was around to blame.

Just you.

And the truth.

You always thought
you were the one
holding it all together.

The reasonable one.

The one who stayed calm.

The one who "tried."

And maybe that's true.

But it's also true
that you got good at deflecting.

At managing perception.

**At telling the story
in a way
that made you look
like the hero.**

You weren't cruel.

You weren't a monster.

But you were avoidant.

You were self-protective.

You were silent
when it mattered.

You weaponized logic
to avoid feeling.

You kept score in your head
and called it fairness.

You're not the villain.

But you're not innocent either.

And now?

You see it.

The patterns.

The defensiveness.

The way you shaped the narrative
to avoid the pain
of being wrong.

It's disorienting.

To realize
you weren't just hurt
you were also hurting someone.

**To see
how your control
was a kind of violence.**

To see
how your silence
was complicity.

To see
how you thought you were "communicating,"

but really
you were just managing fallout.

But let me tell you something:

This moment
this terrifying,
ego-shattering moment

is sacred.

Because only the honest ones
get here.

Only the brave.

Only the ones
willing to lose the story
in order to find the truth.

You don't need
to drown in shame.

You need to stay.

Stay with the discomfort.

Stay with the knowing.

Let it work you.

Let it change you.

You are not irredeemable.

You are not a lost cause.

You are a human being

and part of being human
is learning
how you've failed others
and how you've failed yourself.

You can clean this up.

Not with perfection.

Not with a hundred apologies
no one asked for.

But with presence.

With change.

With the quiet decision
to become someone safer

even if no one's watching.

This is how healing begins:

Not by declaring yourself good,

but by staying in the room
long enough
to become someone better.

You're still welcome at the table.

Even now.

Especially now.

—The Sun

Letter 83: To the One Who Played Both Sides

You weren't always
the villain.

But you weren't always
the victim either.

You've been
the one crying
in the wreckage

and the one
who pulled the pin.

You know
what it's like
to be betrayed.

To be left,
lied to,
let down.

To carry
the grief of
how dare you.

And the grief of
how could I?

That's a special kind of ache,
isn't it?

To realize
you are not just the wounded.

**But also the one
who wounded.**

Not just the loyal one.

But the one
who disappeared
when it mattered most.

Some days
you try to make sense
of the ledger.

Stack your sins
against your scars.

Try to explain,
excuse,
or outgrow it all.

Try to make it neat.

It's never neat.

You want to be better.

You are trying.

And that's not nothing.

**But sometimes
trying
doesn't undo the damage.**

Sometimes
the apology
has to live inside your actions,

because the person you hurt
doesn't want your words.

And you
have to live with that.

This is the grief
of growing up.

Of seeing yourself whole
not heroic.

Of realizing
that the stories you've told
about who you are

need to be rewritten
in a harder,
truer voice.

And still

**you're allowed
to love yourself.**

Not in a cheap,
self-forgiving way.

But in a bone-deep,
honest one.

You're allowed
to walk forward.

Just don't pretend
you didn't do
what you did.

Don't pretend
you didn't feel
what you felt.

Don't pretend
your pain
makes you innocent.

And don't pretend
your guilt
makes you unworthy.

You are both.

You are the one
who fucked around.

You are the one
who got scorched.

You are the one
who knows now.

So carry it all.

With humility.

With grief.

With grace.

And let the weight
of what you've lived

make you someone
worth becoming.

—The Sun

Letter 84: To the One Who Became The Break In The Bloodline

You didn't mean
to be the rupture.

You weren't trying
to start a war.

You just couldn't
keep pretending.

Pretending
that silence
was safety.

That loyalty
meant agreement.

**That love
required you
to shrink.**

So you said
the thing no one said.

You became the first
to name the wound.

The first to say
I don't want to pass this on.

The first
to love them
but not like that.

Not
at the cost
of yourself.

And in doing so,
you broke something.

Maybe not on purpose.

But with precision.

The illusion.

The inheritance.

The unspoken agreement
that said
this is just how we are.

Now you carry
two griefs:

**The grief of what they did.
And the grief of what you lost
when you told the truth.**

Because you lost something,
didn't you?

A seat at the table.

The easy version of family.

The comfort
of not knowing
what you know now.

You became
the one they don't understand.

The one they talk about sideways.

The one
who made it awkward.

But you also became
the beginning.

Of tenderness.

Of truth.

Of a lineage
that doesn't eat its own
to feel whole.

You are not
the shame
of the family.

You are
the reckoning.

And even if no one thanks you

Even if you walk alone
for a while

The break you made
is the space
where something holy
can begin.

—The Sun

Letter 85: To the One Who Clings To Superiority

Maybe you were taught
that your worth
was measured
by where you stood
in the order.

Smarter.
Stronger.
Faster.
Better.

Maybe someone made you believe
you were supposed to lead.

Supposed to win.

Supposed to be right.

And when that stopped
being true
when the world didn't hand you
the crown
you were promised

something cracked.

But instead of grieving it,
you doubled down.

You sharpened your voice.

You tightened your grip.

You kept telling the story
that you were above,

because you didn't know
who you'd be
if you weren't.

That's not strength.

**That's fear
wearing pride
as armor.**

It's okay
to be afraid.

It's okay
to feel the ache
of not being the center
anymore.

It's okay
to want to be seen,
to matter,
to have your story honored.

But superiority
won't give you that.

It only isolates you.

Because the moment
you put yourself above,

you've already stepped away
from love.

From empathy.
From humility.
From learning.
From humanity.

This isn't shame.

It's an invitation.

To grieve
what was never yours
to begin with.

To let go
of the myth

that you're worth more
than anyone else.

To become human
again.

No titles.
No thrones.

Just a heart
trying,
like the rest of us,

to belong.

—The Sun

Letter 86: To the One Who Stayed Too Long

You knew.

Long before the end,
long before the excuses
turned to silence
and the waiting
turned to withering

you knew.

But you kept making yourself forget.

You rehearsed the good moments
like they were proof.

You clung to potential
like it was a promise.

You watered dead things
because no one taught you
that love isn't supposed to be
self-erasure.

You stayed.

Not because you were weak,
but because you were hopeful.

Because you believed in trying.

Because leaving felt like failure
and failure felt like a shame
you didn't want to carry.

You told yourself
you were being loyal.

Being mature.

Being forgiving.

But the truth was sharper:

You were afraid.

Afraid of hurting them.
Afraid of being alone.
Afraid of what it would mean
to admit
that you were starving
in plain sight.

So you shrank.

You twisted yourself
into something

smaller,
quieter,
more agreeable.

You called it "compromise."

**But really,
it was grief.**

And now?

You carry a different ache.

The one that says:
"I knew better.
And I stayed anyway."

So let me say what no one else will:

You don't have to hate yourself
for staying.

You don't have to rewrite the past
to make sense of it.

You don't have to turn your hope
into a weapon.

You loved.
You tried.

And when it became clear
that trying was killing you

you eventually chose yourself.

That is not failure.
That is resurrection.

So bury the guilt.
Mourn the time.

But don't you dare confuse
endurance
with worth.

You are not late.

You are just in bloom
now that there's finally light.

—The Sun

Letter 87: To the One Who Finally Said "This Isn't Enough"

You said it softly at first.

In the bathroom.

In your car.

In a whisper
you didn't think counted yet.

"This isn't enough."

But even then,
your body heard it.

Your life felt it.

Your soul
started packing its bags.

Because once you say it
even once

the truth starts
to rearrange the furniture.

It gets louder.
More insistent.

More unwilling to let you settle for crumbs
and call it a meal.

You tried to take it back.

You made the list of pros and cons.

You told yourself
you were lucky.

You reminded yourself
that other people have it worse.

But still,
it came back.

"This isn't enough."

Not because you're ungrateful.
Not because you're unrealistic.

But because you finally stopped
gaslighting yourself
into accepting a life
that doesn't feed you.

And here's the part no one tells you

when you say it out loud?

People will flinch.

They'll tell you
you're selfish.
Dramatic.
Hard to please.

They'll warn you about the risk.
The fallout.
The loneliness.

But what they really mean is:
"How dare you want more than survival?"
"How dare you stop pretending this is fine?"

You didn't say, "This is nothing."

You said, "It's not enough."

And that's a sacred line in the sand.

That's where numbness ends
and aliveness begins.

So let the world call it dramatic.
Let them call it impulsive.
Let them call it anything they want.

You're not here
to play the role
of the grateful ghost.

You're here
to live.

And now that you've said it

now that your soul has heard it

the rest of your life begins.

—The Sun

Letter 88: To the One Who Let It Burn So They Could Be Reborn

You didn't walk away.

You set it on fire.

Not out of hatred.
Not out of vengeance.

But because you finally understood:
Some things only die
if you stop feeding them.

So you stopped.

Stopped explaining.
Stopped fixing.
Stopped pretending your peace
was worth less than their comfort.

And it burned.

God, it burned.

Your plans.
Your identities.
Your reputation.

**The version of you
that tried to keep it all together
while quietly disintegrating.**

You lost people.
You lost approval.
You lost the illusion
that being good
would keep you safe.

But in the ashes?

You found breath.
You found quiet.

You found the first yes
that ever felt real.

Let them say you're selfish.
Let them say you changed.
Let them say you ruined everything.

They're right.

You did ruin everything
that was slowly ruining you.

You did not "fall apart."
You dismantled the cage.

You walked barefoot
through the blaze.

You gave your former self
a funeral
and didn't apologize for surviving.

That's not destruction.
That's divinity.

So if the grief still stings
let it.

If the loneliness feels like a void
trust it.

That emptiness is sacred.

It's space you cleared
so truth could finally grow there.

You are not lost.
You are between versions.

And the one who's coming?

doesn't flinch.
doesn't beg.
doesn't explain.

She just becomes.

—The Sun

Letter 89: To the One Who Walked Away From What Everyone Else Called Perfect

They didn't get it.

How could they?

From the outside,
it looked ideal.

The job.
The partner.
The house.
The timeline.

You made it.
You had it.

And then
you left.

You walked away
from the dream
everyone else was still chasing.

The one you were supposed
to be grateful for.

The one you spent years building.

The one that made other people say,
"I wish I had your life."

But you knew.

It wasn't your life.

It was a costume.
A well-tailored,
socially approved,
perfectly respectable cage.

And the truth is
it didn't die suddenly.

It eroded.
Bit by bit.

With every moment
you smiled
when you wanted to scream.

Every time you said "I'm fine"
when your body whispered "I'm not."

Every dream you downsized.
Every truth you swallowed.

And then one day,
you realized:

this "perfect" life
required you to disappear.

So you did the unthinkable.

You left comfort for truth.
Stability for soul.
Image for integrity.

And it wrecked you.

The loneliness.
The doubt.
The silence from people
who only loved you
when you made sense to them.

But even in the ache
you knew.

You had finally chosen yourself.

They don't have to understand.

It wasn't their life to live.
It wasn't their soul at stake.

You did not walk away
from something perfect.

You walked away
from something performative.

And in doing so,
you gave yourself the chance
to be real.

That's not failure.
That's freedom.

—The Sun

Letter 90: To the One Who Started Telling the Truth and Lost Everything, But Found Themselves

It didn't happen all at once.

It started small.

A quiet "no"
where you used to say "sure."

A pause
instead of a performance.

A shift in your voice
when you stopped pretending
you didn't care.

You didn't mean to
burn it all down.

You were just trying to be honest.

To finally say what was real.

To stop editing your soul
for the comfort of others.

**But people don't always like the truth
especially when it disrupts
their version of you.**

So they left.
Or turned cold.
Or called you selfish.
Or said you'd changed.

And maybe you had.

Maybe the old you
the agreeable one,
the quiet one,
the polished one
was finally dead.

Because here you are now:

Stripped.
Exposed.
Unapologetic.

Alone, maybe
but you're here.

You stopped lying to survive.

Stopped shrinking to fit.

Stopped bleeding for rooms
that only loved you
when you played small.

And yes, it cost you.

The friendships.
The job.
The version of family
that required your silence.
The false peace.

But look at what you found:

Your spine.
Your voice.
Your actual fucking life.

You're not crazy.
You're just finally awake.

And the world that once felt safe?

It was only safe
because you kept
abandoning yourself
to stay in it.

That's not safety.
That's captivity.

You're free now.

Not comfortable.
Not approved.
Not always understood.

But free.

And when you build from that place

what stays will see you.

What grows will know you.

What loves you
will choose the real you.

You didn't lose everything.

You lost what wasn't meant
for the honest version of you.

And that version?

They're not going back.

Welcome home.

—The Sun

Letter 91: To the One Who's Done Explaining Their Needs

You didn't start out angry.

You started out hopeful.
Generous.
Patient.

You gave
the benefit of the doubt.

You gave
second chances.

You gave
detailed explanations,
annotated with kindness,
in the language of someone else's comfort.

But kindness without return
turns into exhaustion.

And now?

You're tired in a way
that no amount of sleep
can fix.

Because you've been making yourself
digestible.
Palatable.
Easier to carry.

**You've bent yourself
into shapes they could understand
or at least tolerate.**

And still, somehow,
it was too much.

Too sensitive.
Too direct.

Too emotional.
Too much you.

So you learned
how to ask without asking.

How to suggest
instead of need.

How to disguise a boundary
as a casual preference.

And you called it
maturity.
You called it
compromise.

But really?

It was survival.

Now, the switch has flipped.

The part of you
that used to explain,
soothe,
convince

it's gone quiet.

Not bitter. Just done.

Done apologizing
for needing rest.

**Done translating your pain
for people who only listen
when it's convenient.**

Done shrinking the size of your "no"
so they'll still think you're nice.

There's no tantrum in this departure.
No dramatic exit.

Just a locked door
they never thought
you'd close.

And maybe they'll say
you've changed.

They'll say
you're cold now.

They'll say
you're distant.

Let them.

They never really knew
how much it took
for you to stay warm
in their winter.

Here's the truth:

You're not too much.
You're not broken.
You're not asking
for anything outrageous.

You're just done
begging to be met.

Your needs are not a
burden.
Your truth is not an
inconvenience.
Your wholeness is not
negotiable.

And the ones who deserve you?

They won't need a PowerPoint to understand you.

They'll just get it. And meet you there.

—The Sun

Letter 92: To the One Who Could No Longer Pretend Everything Was Fine

You held it together
for longer than anyone knows.

With a smile.
With a spreadsheet.
With a perfectly reasonable explanation
for why you were just tired.

You got so good at functioning
that even you forgot
you were breaking.

You answered every
"How are you?"
with
"I'm good!"

You made jokes
at the right time.
You celebrated
everyone else's milestones.
You texted back
with emojis.
You kept it moving.

And all the while,
your insides were coming apart
like a seam
that no one bothered to stitch.

But the world loves a functional person.

Especially one
who doesn't ask for much.

Especially one
who looks impressive on paper.

Especially one

who never complains
at least not out loud.

So you did what was expected.

You made yourself
smaller than the truth.

You managed your grief
like a project.

You rationed your hope
so no one would call you naïve.

You swallowed your disappointment
so often
it stopped tasting bitter.

Just numb.

Until one day,
you couldn't do it anymore.

It wasn't a breakdown.
It wasn't a crisis.
It was a click.

A door in your chest
slamming shut.

A voice inside that whispered
not cruelly,
but clearly

Enough.

Enough pretending this is sustainable.
Enough pretending the marriage is fine.
Enough pretending the job is your purpose.
Enough pretending the friendships still feed you.
Enough pretending you don't care.

The truth came.

Not as a scream.
But as a stillness
you couldn't unhear.

And now?

You're not hiding.

Not from yourself.

Not from the people
who only loved the version of you
that didn't need anything.

Not from the life
you're finally admitting isn't working.

You're not crazy
for unraveling.

You're not broken
for wanting more.

You're not selfish
for choosing honesty
over harmony.

This is not your failure.

This is your threshold.

And yes
it will cost you.

The performance
always does.

But what you get back?

Is breath.
Is clarity.
Is self-respect.

Is a life
that feels like something you chose
not just something
you inherited.

Let them be confused.
Let them whisper.
Let them wonder
why you changed.

You didn't.

You just stopped pretending.

And now, finally
you're free.

—The Sun

Letter 93: To the One Who Disappeared Without Meaning To

It felt
like a stumble.

You stopped showing up.
Didn't answer texts.
Missed birthdays.

Stopped trying
to keep up
with everyone else's noise.

You told yourself
you were just tired.
Just overwhelmed.

But somewhere
beneath the excuses
was something truer:

You were breaking.

And something in you knew
you needed to be alone for that.

You didn't make
a big announcement.
No dramatic exits.

You just... slipped.
Quietly.
Without fanfare.

And for a while,
maybe you felt guilt about that.
Maybe you still do.

But let's name
what actually happened:

You gave yourself
back to yourself.

Without permission.
Without applause.
Without knowing
if you'd ever come back the same.

You slowed down
enough
to hear what hurt.

You stopped performing.

You stopped pretending to be okay
just because everyone else
needed you to be.

And somewhere
in that unplanned retreat,
you found a strange kind of peace.

Not the kind you post about.
Not the kind anyone else understands.

But the kind
that wraps around your bones and says,

"Stay.
Just a little longer.
Let the world miss you
for once."

Now
you're surfacing again.

Not because someone asked you to.
But because your voice
is ready to carry.

Because the stillness
gave you something
the world never could:

Yourself.

So come gently.
Come real.

Don't rush the re-entry.

And don't forget:

**You don't have to explain
where you've been.**

You just have to decide
where you want to go next.

—The Sun

Letter 94: To the One Who's Still Gone

You didn't vanish
to make a point.

You left
because being seen
started to hurt.

Because the noise
didn't feel like music
anymore.

Because the world
became a place
where you had to wear armor
just to say hello.

So you stopped showing up.

Stopped offering pieces
of yourself
to people who only wanted
the edges.

You didn't announce it.
You just... withdrew.

And here's what no one talks about:
**Sometimes not coming back
is holy.**

Sometimes staying gone
off-grid,
offline,
under wraps
is the most honest thing
you can do.

Because you're not avoiding life.
You're letting life reform you
in private.

And maybe you'll return, someday.

Maybe the world will feel
safe enough again.

Maybe someone will say your name
in just the right tone

and you'll remember
who you are out loud.

But maybe not.
Maybe this quiet isn't a pause
it's the new tempo.

You don't owe anyone an update.
You don't have to be "better"
to be worthy of company.
You don't have to reappear
for the sake of appearances.

If you're still gone,
if the retreat still feels like refuge
Stay.

This isn't avoidance.
It's reclamation.

You're not lost.
You're becoming.

—The Sun

Letter 95: To the One Who Doesn't Feel Like Talking Anymore

You're not
upset.

You're not
cold.

You're not
unraveling.

You're just tired
and not the kind of tired
that sleep can fix.

Tired of explaining
what feels obvious.
Tired of shrinking
what you really mean
just to make it easier
for other people to hear.

You used to talk more.

Used to share,
update,
fill the space.

But lately, even the simple "how are you?" feels like a trap.
Because how do you answer honestly
without scaring someone off?

There's nothing wrong with you.

You're just learning
to value your voice
enough

not to throw it into empty rooms.

It's okay to go quiet.
It's okay to speak
only when you're ready,
and not because
the silence makes someone else uncomfortable.

Your quiet doesn't
mean you're broken.

It means you're listening
to yourself.
And that kind of listening is sacred.

So take your time.

Say nothing if you want.

The people who deserve you
will never demand you at full volume
(unless you want to be).

–The Sun

Letter 96: To the One Who Always Says "Maybe"

There was a time
when you said yes
without thinking.

Yes
to the dinner.
Yes
to the call.
Yes
to the version of yourself that could stay up late
and still carry the weight in the morning.

You were always available.

Always reachable.

Always "down for whatever."

**And slowly,
without meaning to,
that started to
hollow you out.**

Because
no one noticed when *you* were tired.
Because
showing up didn't mean you were seen.
Because
being there wasn't the same as *being met*.

So now,
you say
maybe.

Not because you're unsure.
But because you've started

to count the cost.

You've learned that presence has a price.
And sometimes,
the price is too high.

Sometimes it's your bandwidth.
Sometimes it's your softness.

Sometimes
it's your ability
to breathe in a room
that doesn't know
how to hold your full weight.

And still, there's grief in it.

Grief for the version of you who could power through.

Grief for how easily you used to belong.

Grief for the way saying yes used to feel like connection
instead of performance.

Now, *maybe* is your shield.
It's the space between
instinct and
obligation.

It's where you check in
with your own body
before handing it over
to anyone else.

You're not unreliable.

You're just in repair.

And this time,
you're making sure that when you show up
it's with your whole self.

Not just the part that knows how to smile through it.

–The Sun

Letter 97: To The One Who's Tired Of Small Talk

You're not unfriendly.
You're not cold.

You're just...
done pretending
to care about things
that don't touch the soul.

"How's work?"
"Crazy weather, huh?"
"What are you watching lately?"
You answer.
Politely.
You nod.
You smile.

But underneath it,
something aches.

Not because the conversation is bad
but because it's *missing.*

Missing depth.

Missing realness.

Missing the moment
where someone says
what they *actually* mean,
instead of circling it
like a plane that never lands.

You don't want to know what someone does.

You want to know what keeps them awake at night.

What they're grieving but haven't said out loud.
Where they go when they feel like disappearing.

You're not better than anyone.
You're just...
hungry for something real.

And that hunger changes things.

It makes you quieter in crowds.
It makes you skip events.
It makes you wonder
if anyone else notices the absence
hiding inside all the noise.

There's grief in this too.

Grief for how rare it's become
to sit across from someone
and feel like *you're both actually here.*

So if you've started talking less,

if you've stopped trying to force connection
through weather reports and work gossip

good.

You're not jaded.
You're just honest.

And the next time someone meets you with realness
when their eyes don't look past you
and their words don't float above you
you'll know.

You'll feel your chest soften.

You'll stop scanning the exits.

And you'll think: *finally.*

–The Sun

Letter 98: To the One Who's Still Themselves, But Quieter Now

You didn't change.
Not in the way people think.

You're still you.
Still thoughtful.
Still quick to laugh
when it's real.
Still full of stories
you don't always feel like telling.

But something shifted.

Not a collapse.
Not a crisis.

Just... a *turning down.*

Of volume.
Of access.

Of the part of you
that used to fill every silence
so no one felt awkward.

There was a time you were the loudest in the room.
Not always in sound,
but in effort.
You carried the mood.
You filled the group chat.
You made things easier
for everyone but yourself.

Now?

Now you let the pauses breathe.
Now you leave some messages on read.
Now you let other people
carry the weight of connection,
and you watch to see
who actually tries.

You're not bitter.
You're not fading.

You're just *recalibrating*
what your presence costs
and who's willing to meet it.

And yes, there's grief in the quiet.

Grief for
the version of you that tried so hard to be undeniable.

Grief for
the friendships that didn't survive the silence.

Grief for
the parts of your identity that were built in service to being liked.

But underneath that grief is *relief.*

You don't need to be the spark anymore.
You've become the fire.

And the people who still get to stand close?
They're the ones who noticed the difference
and *stayed anyway.*

–The Sun

Letter 99: To the One Who Keeps Dimming Themselves to Be Chosen

You shrink.

Not all at once.

Not dramatically.

Just a little at a time.

You swallow the urge
to say what you really think.
You pretend you're fine
with "casual."
You laugh at jokes that
make your chest tighten.

You get smaller, softer, simpler
so no one feels overwhelmed.
Because somewhere along the way,
you learned that too much light
makes people leave.

So you lower your voice.
Hide your hunger.
Tame your brilliance.
And call it compatibility.

You want to be loved.
But not at the cost of being left again.

So you audition.
Without realizing it.

You give them the version they can handle.

You hand over the safe,

sweet,
sparkly parts.
The palatable bits.
The low-maintenance love.

And it works.
They stay.
They like you.

They say you're "easy to be with."
But deep down, you know the truth.
They don't know you.

Not really.

They've never seen the whole storm.
The teeth of your desire.
The parts of you that won't
bend to be kept.

And you keep wondering
why it still feels lonely
even when you're not alone.

Here's why:
**Love built on performance
is just another form
of self-abandonment.**

You were not made to be tolerable.

You were made to be true.
All the way.
Even if it costs you people
who only loved the echo of you.

So stop shrinking.

Stop sandpapering your soul down to fit.
Stop asking,
"Will they still want me if I don't dim?"

The ones who are meant for you
will not flinch
in the full glare of your light.

You don't need to be chosen
for half of who you are.

Let yourself be known.
And if they walk away?

Let them.

You are not here to audition.

You are here to burn.

—The Sun

Intentionally left blank. Use for notes, if needed.

Interlude

Letter 100: To the One Who Feels Like They're Between Lives

You're not where you were.
But you're not where you're going yet,
either.

You've shed the skin,
buried the version of you
that once knew how to survive here.

But nothing new has rooted.
Not yet.

You're floating.
Suspended.
Still moving,
technically
but nothing touches.

Every conversation feels
half a second off.
Every decision feels like dress-up.
Even your face in the mirror
looks like someone mid-shift.

You're not broken.
You're just between.

Between identities.
Between dreams.
Between
roles,
relationships,
gods,
griefs.

Between the life that was never quite right
and the one that hasn't landed yet.

You don't need to rush this.

You're not behind.

This in-between is not a failure of arrival
it's a sacred passage.

The seed doesn't sprout

the second it's planted.

It breaks open in the dark.

It waits.

It learns the texture of soil.

It gathers force.

You are not stalled.
You are gathering force.

And when your next life calls

when the roots break

through the shell

and something green

finally climbs toward light
it will be because you

let this moment stretch
as long as it needed to.

Even here, in the strange in-between,
you are becoming.

—The Sun

Part V: Ash & Bloom

Some things had to die.
Some things had to burn.
Some illusions couldn't come with you.

This part of the story is what grew out of the smoke
the soft green after the fire,
the bloom that learned to root in ash.

This is where the haunted parts of you made peace with the living ones.
Where you stopped running.
Where you let it hurt *and* let it open you.

Not a return to who you were.
But a return to something *older.*
Something *truer.*
Something buried beneath the performance.

You didn't just survive.
You bloomed.

Letter 101: To the One Who Came Back to Life

You didn't announce it.
No parade.
No dramatic return.

Just a quiet breath
in the middle of a regular day
when something flickered again
not joy,
not peace,
not purpose exactly.
Just...presence.

For the first time in a long time,
you noticed your own aliveness.

Maybe it was a song.

Maybe it was the way
the light hit your kitchen counter.

Maybe it was the way
you laughed
not politely,
but from the gut.

And you realized:
You were still in there.

After all the years
you went numb just to function,
after all the masks
you wore so you wouldn't scare people,

after all the days
you kept your grief
in your throat
like a swallowed scream
you remembered what it felt like
to want something.

Not out of desperation.
Not out of survival.
But because something in you
was ready again.

Ready to feel.
Ready to risk softness.
Ready to try
without the promise
of applause or perfection.

You didn't rebuild overnight.
You didn't light candles
and chant affirmations
until the pain disappeared.

You dragged yourself back,
one ugly truth,
one honest no,
one boundary at a time.

And every time
you told the truth
instead of performing,
you came back a little more.

Every time
you chose rest without guilt,
you stitched another piece
of your spirit back in.

Every time
you let yourself long
for something without shame,
you cracked the window
just wide enough
for a little air to get in.

This letter isn't for the version of you
that still thinks they have to prove
they're healed.

It's for the you who already knows:

Wholeness was never the goal.
Reunion was.
With yourself.

Welcome back.
You didn't miss your life.
It waited.

—The Sun

Letter 102: To the One Who Finally Let Themselves Be Seen

You almost didn't.

For years,
you stayed shapeshifted.

Polite.
Measured.
Easy to digest.

You kept it light.
Kept it nice.
Kept it
survivable.

You wore versions of yourself
like armor.

The agreeable one.
The high achiever.
The peacekeeper.

The one who never needed too much.
The one who made
everyone else
comfortable.

You weren't hiding
because you were weak.

**You were hiding
because the world taught you
it wasn't safe
to be real.**

Not with your feelings.
Not with your edges.
Not with the truth
of your hunger.

So you mastered
the art
of vanishing
in plain sight.

Always present.
Rarely known.

But something shifted.

Maybe the mask cracked.
Maybe the ache got too loud.
Maybe you just
got tired
of carrying
the lie.

Either way

you stopped performing.

You let it slip
the sadness,
the joy,
the *you*.

And you didn't die.

You didn't get left.

You didn't unravel
into nothingness
like your fear said you would.

Instead,
someone looked at you
and didn't flinch.

Didn't fix.
Didn't flee.

They just
saw you.

354

And that moment?

It did something
permanent.

Because once
you've been met
in your realness

you can't go back
to counterfeit connection.

You can't un-know
what it feels like
to be witnessed
without needing to shrink
or shine.

That doesn't mean
it's always safe.

Doesn't mean
everyone
will handle your truth
well.

But now you know:

**Being seen
is survivable.**

Even sacred.

So if the voice comes back

the one that says
"you're too much,"
or
"you're too messy,"
or
"they won't understand"

remember this:

You are not here
to be palatable.

You are not here
to play a role.

You are not here
to perform your pain
in a prettier font.

You are here
to be felt.

Fully.

You are here
to be known.

Keep showing up.

Even if your hands shake.
Even if your voice breaks.

You are worth
being witnessed.

—The Sun

Letter 103: To the One Who Remembered What They Loved

You almost
left it behind.

Not on purpose
just the way people lose things
when life
demands everything.

The thing that used to
light you up.

The small ritual.
The ridiculous dream.

The song
that made you feel
infinite.

The color
that made you bold.

The version of you
that used to laugh
without checking
the room
first.

You didn't forget it
all at once.

It faded.

Got scheduled over.
Got labeled
impractical,
childish,
indulgent.

Got buried
under the grind
and the bills

and the mask
you wore
to keep going.

But one day,
without fanfare,
you remembered.

Maybe you saw
someone else do it.
Maybe it came
in a dream.
Maybe it was just
a sudden ache

like your soul
knocking
from the inside.

And instead of
brushing it off

you followed it.

You played.
You wrote.
You danced.

You built something
no one asked for.

**You made the thing
for no reason
except that
it called to you.**

And you remembered:

You are allowed
to love things

without monetizing them.
Without explaining them.
Without being good at them.

Without needing
anyone else
to understand.

This world
will try to make you believe
that usefulness
is the same
as worth.

That if something
doesn't scale,
doesn't sell,
doesn't solve
a problem

it's not worth
your time.

But here's the truth:

**What you love
is sacred.**

Even if it's small.
Especially
if it's small.

You don't need a reason
to return to yourself.

You just need
to say
yes.

So make the thing.
Buy the book.
Take the walk.

Paint your nails
like the sky.

Play the music
that makes no sense

to anyone
but your heart.

It matters.

Because *you*
matter.

And you're allowed
to be in love
with your life
again.

Start there.

Start now.

—The Sun

Letter 104: To the One Who Needed Proof That Magic Still Lives in a Body Like Yours

You were taught
to be suspicious
of yourself.

To mistrust
the curve,
the softness,
the stretch.

To believe
that beauty had rules.
That worth
had dimensions.

That certain bodies
were invitations

and yours
was a warning.

You learned
how to tuck your hunger
into politeness.

How to apologize
without words.

How to endure
the glances,
the jokes,
the quiet exclusions

and still
show up.

**You were trained
to be grateful
for scraps.**

To interpret neglect
as neutrality.

To think
"strong"
meant silent.

To think
"beautiful"
meant thin.

To think
"enough"
meant invisible.

But here's the truth
no one profits
from you remembering:

**Magic
has never been
about symmetry.**

It doesn't worship
collarbones.

It doesn't need
your waist
to vanish.

It needs
your aliveness.

Your breath.
Your blood.

Your
fucking
fire.

**The people who told you otherwise
were wrong.**

They mistook
conformity
for safety.

And safety
for love.

But love
doesn't shrink you.

Love
sees you.

Love
stays.

And what if
the parts they taught you
to hate

the thighs,
the belly,
the nose,
the voice,
the hair

**were never flaws
but frequencies?**

What if
you are not a mistake
to be fixed,

but a signal
trying to come through?

This letter
is for the body
they underestimated.

The one
that danced
anyway.

That kept living.
That keeps
trying.

You are not
too much.

You are not
too late.

You are not
alone.

You
are the spell.

XOXO,
The Sun

Letter 105: To the One Who Forgave Themselves for Surviving

You made it.

Not because it was easy.
Not because you were stronger.

But because you had to.

Because there was
no other option.

Because the alternative
was collapse

and you didn't have
the luxury.

So you survived.

By bracing.
By hardening.
By becoming
what the moment demanded.

You smiled
when you wanted to scream.

You held it together
when no one else did.

You cleaned up messes
you didn't make.

You became responsible
for things
that should've
never
been yours.

And somewhere
along the way

you started to believe
that survival
made you less pure.

Less lovable.
Less worthy.

Because you coped
in ways
you don't want to talk about.

Because you shut down
instead of falling apart.

Because you got good
at pretending.

Because some days,
you still do.

You've carried shame
like a second skin.

For not speaking up.
For not leaving sooner.
For needing
what you needed
just to stay alive.

But here's the thing:

You made it.

And that's not a sin.

That's
a miracle.

**Survival
is not a moral failure.**

It's not a flaw.
It's not proof
that you did it wrong.

It's proof
you knew
how to stay alive
in a world
that didn't always care
if you did.

**You don't need
to keep apologizing
for the parts of you
that did what they had to.**

You don't have to
keep punishing yourself
for not being soft
in a time
that required armor.

Forgiveness
is not saying
it was okay.

It's saying
you're okay now.

It's saying:

"I see what you did
to protect me.

And I thank you.

But you don't have to
run the show anymore."

Let the war inside you
be over.

Let the self-blame
unhook from your ribs.

Let the story
be true
without being damning.

You're not who you were.

You're
who survived.

And that version of you?

They deserve
a place
at the table, too.

—The Sun

Letter 106: To the One Who's Rebuilding From the Ashes

There was fire.

Maybe
you set it.

Maybe
life did.

Maybe it just
caught
one day

quiet at first,
then raging.

**Either way,
it burned through
everything
you thought would last.**

The job.
The marriage.
The illusion.

The version of you
that kept trying
to hold it all
together.

Now
you're standing
in the after.

Still breathing, somehow.
Still here.

But everything
looks different.

Smells
like smoke.

Sounds
like silence.

And the ground beneath you
feels fragile,

like it might give out
if you move
too fast.

You're rebuilding.

But not
from blueprints.

From instinct.
From scar tissue.

From the wreckage
of what couldn't be saved

**and the stubborn hope
that something better
can still rise.**

Some people
won't understand.

They'll look
at your new beginning
and call it
a setback.

They'll ask
why you left.
Why you changed.
Why you had to
burn it down
at all.

Smile,
if you want.

But don't answer.

They weren't there
the night
the match was lit.

You were.

And you knew:

If you didn't let it fall apart,
it would take
you
with it.

So now?

You get to build
something that fits.

Not something impressive.
Not something
that proves
a point.

**Something that feels
like truth.**

Even if it's small.
Even if it's slow.
Even if it looks
nothing like
what you had
before.

You're allowed
to build gently.

To rest
when you're tired.

To honor
the grief
between the bricks.

Because this isn't just
reconstruction.

It's resurrection.

And this time?

You don't owe anyone
a masterpiece.

Only something real.
Only something
yours.

**Only something
that lets you
come home
to yourself.**

The flames
took a lot.

But they didn't
take you.

—The Sun

Letter 107: To the One Who's Still Carrying What No One Saw

It didn't
look like trauma.

It didn't come
with bruises
or blood.

No headlines.
No arrests.

Just
moments.

Small,
quiet
moments

that rewired
your nervous system

without
anyone noticing.

You were
the "resilient" one.

The responsible one.
The one
who could take it.

So you did.

You carried
the chaos.

You carried
the secrets.

You carried
the silence after the scream,
the tension in the air,

the things
that were "normal"
in your house

but made your stomach ache
for no reason.

You didn't collapse.

You adapted.

You became
hyper-aware.
Hyper-capable.
Hyper-independent.

And no one
asked why.

**No one asked
what it cost you
to be the one
who always had it together.**

You smile
in pictures.
You show up
to work.
You answer
the text.

And still

something inside
feels heavy.

Not broken.
Just
burdened

by what was
never named.

So let me name it
for you:

You lived through
things
that required
coping.

You survived
things
that no one
protected you from.

You became
who you needed to be

to stay safe,
loved,
included,
invisible.

And that's not nothing.

That's not weakness.
That's not
being dramatic.

It's grief.

And you
get to have it.

Even if
it wasn't "that bad."

Even if
other people had it worse.

Even if
you can't point to a single moment

and say
that's when it happened.

You are not required
to keep carrying
what no one else
was willing to see.

You are allowed
to name it now.

To lay it down.

To be held
instead of holding it all.

The strength you built
was never meant
to be a life sentence.

You
get to feel now.

You
get to unravel.

You
get to heal.

And no one
has to understand it

for it to be real.

—The Sun

Letter 108: To the One Who's Ready to Try Again

You've been here
before.

The edge.
The threshold.

The trembling moment
between retreat
and return.

You swore
you wouldn't.

You told yourself
you were done.

Done hoping.
Done reaching.
Done setting yourself up
just to get
let down.

You weren't wrong
to stop.

You were
exhausted.

You were
heartbroken.

You were
protecting
what was left
of your spirit.

**But something in you
has shifted.**

Subtly.
Quietly.

Like a small animal
crawling out
after winter.

And now?

You're ready
to try again.

Not with naive eyes.
Not with
a wide-open chest
and no boundaries.

But with a new kind
of courage

the kind
that belongs to people
who've lost before

and still
choose
to begin again.

**Trying again
doesn't mean
forgetting.**

It means remembering
without letting it
calcify.

It means loving
smarter,
not smaller.

It means showing up
with both
discernment
and softness.

It means
refusing
to become bitter

even if
you had every reason
to.

You might still
flinch.

You might still
second-guess.

You might still
brace
for the drop.

That's okay.

You've learned
to walk
with ghosts.

You know how
to move forward
even when
your legs shake.

That's not
weakness.

**That's wisdom
with
muscle memory.**

So try.

Try again.

Start the project.
Reach out first.
Apply
for the thing.

Say the words
you held in
last time.

Let the world
meet
this new version of you

the one who's been burned,
but not buried.

Hope
is not
a betrayal
of your past.

It's a declaration
of your
aliveness.

And you?

**You are
still alive.**

Still here.

Still willing.

That alone
is a miracle.

—The Sun

Letter 109: To the One Who No Longer Shrinks

You used to
apologize
for existing.

Not out loud, maybe

but in the way
you stepped aside.

The way
you kept the pitch
of your voice
soft.

The way you said
"whatever works for you"
**when it
absolutely
did not
work for you.**

You mastered
the art
of smallness.

You became
accommodating.
Agreeable.
Pleasant.

So digestible
that people forgot
you had
teeth.

And when something hurt?

You swallowed it.

When someone
overlooked you?

You told yourself
it wasn't
a big deal.

When your needs
came up?

You buried them
beneath
a smile.

But something broke.

Or maybe
it clicked.

**One day,
you realized
you were starving
in a life
that required
you
to disappear.**

And you said:

No more.

Now?

You take up space.
You speak.
You choose.

You say no.
You say yes
but only
when you mean it.

And not everyone
claps.

Some people
miss the version of you

who made
their lives easier.

Let them.

You didn't come here
to be small.

You didn't incarnate
to be liked
more than you're known.

You didn't fight your way
through all that grief,
all that fire,
all that goddamn
silence

just to be
palatable.

YOU

ARE

BIG.

And you're
not sorry.

You
are
loud.

And you're
not ashamed.

You
are
whole.

And you're finally
home
in your own body.

You're not
too much.

You're just
finally
enough
for yourself.

And that
changes everything.

Don't shrink again.

Don't whisper
when your truth
is a bell tower.

Don't dim
because someone else
is afraid
of your light.

You're not the problem.

You're the proof.

—The Sun

Letter 110: To the One Who Believes They Might Still Belong Here

You've thought
about disappearing.

Not in a headline
kind of way

but in that
quiet,
aching way

that whispers:

maybe the world
wouldn't notice
if I backed out
quietly.

You've felt
like extra.
Like noise.

Like the only one
who didn't get
the manual.

You've watched
people move through life
like they know
what they're doing

**while you've been
white-knuckling
your way
through mornings.**

There were days
you didn't know
how to stay.

Nights
you couldn't find
a single thread
to hold onto.

You wondered
if you were
built wrong

if maybe
your feelings
were a defect,

if maybe
being this sensitive

meant
you weren't made
for Earth.

But you're still here.

Somehow.

Despite everything.

Despite the grief
that had no name.

Despite the years
you lived
as a ghost
in your own story.

Despite the shame.
Despite the silence.

Despite the fact
that no one
ever taught you
how to hold
a soul
this heavy.

You are still here.

And that
matters
more
than you know.

Maybe
you don't believe
in hope.

But you
believe in something.

Something
that made you
keep reading.

Something
that made you
open this book.

Something
that made you whisper

just barely

maybe
I'm not done yet.

So let me say this
clearly.

You
    BELONG
        here.

Not because
you're useful.

Not because
you're fixed.

Not because
you're impressive,
or selfless,
or spiritual.

You belong
because
you're real.

And real things
have a place
in this world

especially
the broken ones.

Especially
the ones
that keep waking up

even
when it hurts.

Stay.

Not because
you owe anyone.

Not because
it gets better
overnight.

But because
there are still
mornings
meant
for you.

Still colors
you haven't seen.

Still moments
holy,

small,
electric

that will remind you
what it means
to be alive.

You're not
out of time.

You're not
unlovable.

You're not
beyond repair.

You're in it.

**And that's
where life
begins
again.**

—The Sun

Letter 111: To the One Who Realized They Can Do Whatever the Fuck They Want

You looked around
one day

and it hit you.

This life?
This body?
This time
you get on Earth?

It's yours.

Not leased.
Not borrowed.
Not assigned to you
with a manual
and a list
of polite roles
to play.

Yours.

And suddenly,
the whole game
started glitching.

The career
you were told
to chase?

Optional.

The version of adulthood
you were sold?

Programmable.

The silent rules
about what's
"respectable,"

"realistic,"
or "enough"?

Breakable.

The people
who made you feel
like you had to shrink
or explain yourself
to be loved?

Replaceable.

You woke up
inside the matrix
of your own life

and realized:

You are the code.
You are the author.

You are not
the supporting cast.

**You are not
obligated
to live
someone else's dream.**

And maybe at first
it felt like too much.

Too much space.
Too much choice.
Too much power
to hold
without a guidebook.

But then
something clicked:

You've always
been allowed.

You just forgot.

So now?

**Now
you are dangerous.**

Because you are no longer
trying
to be digestible.

Because you are done
asking
for permission.

Because you are building
a life
that makes you feel
alive

even if no one else claps.
Even if they don't get it.
Even if it means
walking alone
for a while.

This isn't about rebellion
for its own sake.

It's about
coming home.

To the part of you
that remembers
what it feels like
to be free.

To want something
without apologizing.

To walk into a room
without performing.

To love
what you love
without footnotes.

You're not selfish.
You're not delusional.
You're not
too much.

You're just
awake
now.

And once
you see the game,

you don't
go back

to playing
by the old rules.

Build it
weird.

Build it
loud.

Build it
slow,
soft,
brave,
naked.

But build it **your way.**

Because this life
is yours.

And it always
was.

—The Sun

Parting Words...

You made it.
Not because you finished this book
but because you told the truth somewhere along the way.

You let yourself feel it.
The thing you thought you had to hide.
The part of you that kept whispering,
"It shouldn't be this hard."

You let it speak.

And now?

You're different.
Not fixed.
Not perfect.
But different.

Because something in you remembered:
You are not a machine.
You are not your output.
You are not a problem to solve.

You are a soul.

And your ache is not a flaw
it's a flare.

Let this be the place you stopped numbing.
Let this be the moment you heard yourself again.
Let this be the page where something in you said,
"I want more."

More life.
More softness.
More truth.
More of you.

There is no roadmap from here.
No checklist.
No moral to the story.

But there is this:

You are not alone.
You are not crazy.
You are still on time.
And it is not too late
to come back to life.

But the grief is still yours.
So my only question is this:
You've been witnessed now, so
What are you going to do with it?

If you want to do something
with it right now,
turn the page.

The Return System is waiting.

—**The Sun**

Intentionally left blank. Use for notes, if needed.

THE RETURN SYSTEM™

What to do when the book cracks you open
This is not the end. It's the threshold.
This section is here for after.

After the letter.

After the page.

When your hands are shaking or your chest feels strange or
you can't tell if you're grieving or just broken.

You're not broken.

You're returning.

The Return System™

This section was built for the aftermath. When you've read something that left your body buzzing, your throat tight, or your soul louder than your mouth.

You do not need to be okay to continue. You only need to *stay here*.

This system unfolds in layers. Starting with small stabilizers and progressing to emergency rituals. Use what you need. Leave the rest. Come back if you need to.

All protocols and rites are offered with accessible variations.

Return Rites
Page 401

Short rituals to stabilize, reground, and integrate

These are the softest landings. Use them after a difficult letter, a hard day, or any moment that leaves you unsteady.

- The Field Reboot
- The Breath Ladder
- The Threshold Sit
- The Bodymap Trace
- The Cloak of Permission

Restoration Rites
Page 418

Somatic practices drawn from *The Book of Human Feelings (coming soon)*
Use these when the signal is stronger like when a specific emotion wants to move, but the body doesn't know how.

• The Self-Anointing (Love)
• The Pulse Press (Fear)
• The Mirror Hunger (Longing)
• The Root Lock (Despair)
• The Grief Rocking Chair (Sorrow)

Break Glass Protocols

Page 438

Emergency rites for when emotions flood the system
These protocols are designed for acute moments like panic, shutdown, rage, collapse. Use them when everything feels too loud or too far away.

• Break Glass 1: Overwhelm Protocol
• Break Glass 2: Numbness Protocol
• Break Glass 3: Rage Protocol
• Break Glass 4: Collapse Response
• Break Glass 5: Grief Protocol
• Break Glass 6: Panic Protocol
• Break Glass 7: Longing Protocol
• Break Glass 8: Shame Protocol
• Break Glass 9: I Don't Know What I'm Feeling Protocol

The Myth Of Self-Reliance

Page 477

Sometimes the thing that keeps us silent is shame itself.

• Letter 112: To the One Who Is Ashamed (or Scared) to Ask for Help
• You Are Not Alone: The Grief Statistics Page

Before You Break: A Map For Survival

Page 485

Not a pep talk. A lifeline.
This is a clear, no-jargon, body-honest guide for what to do when you're **really** not okay.

Includes:
• What to say when you don't know what to say
• Accessible hotline options (including Deaf, neurodivergent, and LGBTQ+ resources)

• Text/chat options for nonverbal or speech-disabled readers
• A reminder: You are allowed to get help.

Journaling Pages
Page 492

- Letters That Resonate: Blank journal pages to record letters that stick with you.
- My Letter: Blank pages to write your own letter

Want printable versions? Visit: **www.invisible-grief.com**

RETURN
RITES

What Are Return Rites?

Short rituals to stabilize, reground, and reenter your field

Not all pain is loud.
Some arrives as flicker, fog, or float
a disconnection so quiet it almost goes unnoticed.

Return Rites are bridges back to the body.

They don't require readiness, bravery, or emotional insight.

They're for the moments *after* something stirs:
when the letter ends, the tears dry, or your nervous system starts to blink awake.

They are not solutions.
They are gentle invitations.
They ask only for presence.

What Are They For?

Each Return Rite is designed to:

- Settle your system without suppressing it
- Help you find yourself again, without force
- Make returning feel like belonging, not punishment

Some use breath.
Some use posture.
Some are as simple as touching your own skin.

They are short.
They are sacred.
They are enough.

Return Rites Quick Reference Guide

Choose the one that matches your state or begin anywhere. Variations are included for mobility, sensory, or neurodivergent access.

Rite	Use When…	Page
The Field Reboot	You feel foggy, fragmented, or disconnected from your body	**404**
Field Reboot (Variation)	You need to ground but can't stand, speak, or move much	405
Breath Ladder	You're overwhelmed and need to regulate your breath through pacing and gentle hand tracing	**407**
Breath Ladder (Variation)	Your breathing is shallow, tight, or trauma-triggered and you need a softer, silent approach	408
Threshold Sit	You're in-between states, uncertain, paused, or grieving, and need to feel witnessed	**409**
Threshold Sit (Variation)	You're sensitive to light, sound, or touch and need to recline while being held in stillness	410
Bodymap Trance	You feel disconnected from your physical body and need to return through guided internal contact	**412**
Bodymap Trance (Variation)	You can't physically touch your body but want to return using visualization or with a partner	413
Cloak of Permission	You feel unsafe, uncertain, or ashamed, and need to reclaim permission to take up space	**415**
Cloak of Permission (Variation)	You're highly sensory-sensitive or triggered by touch, and need a gentler form of self-wrapping	416

If none of them call you,
just sit on the threshold.
That counts too.

You are not lost.
You are in the process of returning.

THE FIELD REBOOT

☼ *A short ritual to restore presence and coherence*

When you feel fragmented, foggy, or like you've left your body, you don't need a full ceremony.

You need a field reset.
Return to the anchor points.
Call your name back through the body.

You'll Need

- Your breath
- A seated or standing position
- 1–2 minutes of privacy

Do This

1. **Place one hand over your chest, the other on your belly.**

2. **Say your full name out loud**. Slowly. Once or twice.

3. **Tap your chest gently 5 times with your fingertips.**

4. **Exhale audibly.** Let your shoulders fall.

5. **Press both feet into the floor.**

6. **Name five things you see.**

Aftercare:

Drink water. Wash your hands. Say:
"I'm back. I can choose again."

The Field Reboot (Variation)
☼ *For low-mobility, non-speaking, or low-sensory-capacity moments*

When you cannot move easily,
when speech feels too far away,
when even breath feels unsteady
reboot the field from the inside out.

Your body will understand the signal.

You'll Need

- Your breath
- Awareness of your inner space (or any still place inside you)
- A soft point of focus (like closed eyes or a familiar texture)

Do This

1. **Inhale through your nose for 3 counts.**
   If that feels unsafe, just *feel the shape of an inhale.*

2. **Exhale slowly through pursed lips for 5 counts**
   or sigh, hum, or release in whatever way feels gentle.

3. **Repeat this rhythm 3 times.**
   Let your system feel the pattern.

4. **In your mind, say:**
   "[Your Name], I'm here."
   "I am with you."
   You can whisper it if you want,
   but you don't have to.

5. **Wiggle a toe, blink once, or even *imagine* movement.**
   That is enough.
   That is your signal:
   I am back.

Aftercare

Place your hand somewhere on your body: chest, thigh, arm.
Whisper (or think):
"I made it back."

THE BREATH LADDER

☼ *A somatic tether to regulate intensity and return to center*

When your breath gets shallow,
when your thoughts start racing,
when you're floating above your body
or drowning inside it
build the ladder.
One rung at a time.
Breathe your way back.

You'll Need

- Just your breath
- A quiet(ish) place to pause, seated or reclined

Do This

1. Inhale through your nose for **2 counts**

2. Exhale through your mouth for **4 counts**

3. Inhale for **3 counts**, exhale for **5**

4. Inhale for **4 counts**, exhale for **6**

5. Inhale for **5 counts**, exhale for **7**
   (If at any point it becomes too much, return to the last step that felt safe.)

Aftercare

Place your hand on your chest.
Say: **"I can slow down. I can be here."**

The Breath Ladder (Variation)

☼ *For breath sensitivity, trauma response, or limited lung capacity*

If deep breathing feels unsafe,
if your lungs won't stretch that far,
if breath itself feels like too much
you can still climb.
This ritual is about rhythm, not effort.

You'll Need

- A finger to trace
- A visual cue (optional) like a line on your palm, a piece of string, or a mark on the wall

Do This

1. **Gently trace a straight or curved line with your finger.**
   It can be drawn, imagined, or real.

2. **As you move forward:**
   Inhale softly through your nose (or just feel the gesture of an inhale).

3. **As you trace back:**
   Exhale through pursed lips, like a quiet **shhh**, or release a sigh if easier.

4. **Repeat the tracing five times.**
   Let your breath follow the motion.
   Let the line carry you.

5. **If breath is difficult or uneven, let the tracing alone become the rhythm.**
   You are still on the ladder.

Aftercare

Hold the finger you used to trace.
Say softly, or just think:
"Even this is enough."

THE THRESHOLD SIT

☼ *A witnessing ritual for when you don't know what comes next*

When you're in-between
not who you were,
not yet who you'll be
this sit is for you.

No fixing.
No forcing.
Just witnessing.

You'll Need

- A place to sit (floor, chair, bed—all valid)
- 5–10 minutes of uninterrupted time

Do This

1. **Sit in stillness.** Set no agenda.

2. **Say (aloud or in your mind):**
   "I am at the threshold. I am allowed to not know."

3. **Let your breath arrive without shaping it.**

4. **Notice one thing around you: color, light, temperature.**

5. **Place your hand on your body where you feel the most sensation,** or the least. Stay there.

Aftercare

Say: "I don't have to be ready. I only have to stay."
Drink something warm, if available.

Threshold Sit (Variation)

☼ *For those unable to sit upright, navigating flare-ups, or experiencing sensory overwhelm*

You do not need to sit to enter this ritual.
You can lie down, recline, or wrap yourself in a blanket.
Stillness does not require posture.
Witnessing can happen anywhere.

You'll Need

- A resting position that feels safe
- A sentence to anchor you

Do This

1. **Choose a grounding phrase.**
   Examples:
   - "This is not the end."
   - "Becoming takes time."
   - "Nothing is required of me right now."

2. **Say it aloud if you can,** or just think it once.
   Then close your eyes.

3. **Listen for any inner reaction**, no judgment if there's silence.
   The noticing is the ritual.

4. **If possible, gently press your hands together,
   or place one hand on your chest and one on your belly.**
   If touch is inaccessible, simply breathe.

5. **Rest.**
   Don't fix.
   Don't decide.
   Let the threshold hold you.

Aftercare

Name one thing that is still true.
Examples:
1. **The window is open.**
2. **I am breathing.**
3. **I am here.**

THE BODYMAP TRACE

☼ *A nervous system scan for reorientation and gentle reconnection*

When the world feels far away, when you've floated too far from yourself this ritual brings you back into your own outline.

No performance.
No pressure.
Just come home.

You'll Need

- Just your breath and your body
- Optional: blanket, lotion, or soft fabric

Do This

1. Sit or lie down. Get still. Close your eyes if that feels safe.

2. Slowly trace the outline of your body in your mind—from the crown of your head, around your ears, down your arms, chest, hips, legs, feet.

3. Whisper to each part (or imagine it):
   "This is my ___." (e.g., "This is my shoulder.")

4. If a part feels numb or hard to reach, pause there. Place your hand there if possible.

5. When you've completed your whole body, say:
   "I am all here. Even the quiet parts."

Aftercare

Wrap yourself in something soft.
Say: **"My body is allowed to come back slowly."**

Bodymap Trance (Variation)
☼ *For limited mobility, paralysis, sensory sensitivity, or dissociation*

This version can be done entirely through visualization, internal cueing, or with the gentle, consented touch of a trusted partner.
There is no need to feel every part.
Only to greet what's still yours.

You'll Need

- A quiet space or headphones
- A sentence to guide the scan

Do This

1. **Imagine your body as a glowing shape outlined in light.**
   You do not need to see it perfectly.
   Just start with the idea of your form.

2. **Slowly "light up" each section like turning on a soft string of fairy lights.**
   This can be done in your mind, with your breath, or with a gentle, consensual touch from someone you trust.

3. **As each area comes into awareness, say or think:**
   "You belong. You are here."

4. **Spend extra time on any part that feels dim, numb, or unreachable.**
   You are not doing this wrong.
   Some parts take longer to return.

5. **End with a soft, full-body image.**
   See or sense your whole outline, glowing gently.
   Let it be incomplete if needed.
   This still counts.

Aftercare

If possible, touch something real: a textured object, a cup, a wall.
Say aloud or silently:
"This is my life, and I'm in it."

THE CLOAK OF PERMISSION
☼ A ritual for returning to your own rules after performing for others

When you've been too palatable,
too pleasing,
too small
wrap yourself back in you.

This is a ritual for shedding performance and reclaiming full expression.

You'll Need

- A large cloth, scarf, blanket, or towel
- Optional: mirror

Do This

1. Sit or stand still. Hold the cloth in both hands.

2. Take one breath for every role you've played today: worker, caretaker, friend, performer…and exhale each one.

3. Wrap the cloth around your shoulders like a cloak.

4. Whisper aloud:
   "I am not required to perform to be worthy of care."
   "I give myself permission to be real again."

5. If using a mirror, look into your own eyes and nod once. That is your seal.

Aftercare

Keep the cloak on as long as you need.
Drink something warm.
Let your face be unguarded.

Cloak Of Permission (Variation)

☼ *For sensory sensitivity, trauma response, or limited mobility*

This version of the ritual is for those who cannot, or choose not to, engage with fabric or external tools.
If touch is too much. If sound is too much. If being seen is too much.
The cloak can still come.

You don't need fabric.
You don't even need to see it clearly.
Just name the intention.
The cloak will know what to do.

You'll Need

- Your breath
- A quiet moment
- (Optional: your imagination, clarity not required)

Do This

1. **Close your eyes** (if safe to do so).
   Imagine a cloak of light forming behind you, this can be blurry, abstract, or felt instead of seen.

2. **With each inhale, let it move closer.**
   With each exhale, let it wrap more fully.

3. No need to rush.
   No need to force the image.
   Just allow it.

4. **Say aloud or in your mind:**
      "I release the roles."
      "I reclaim myself."

5. **Let the imagined weight settle on your shoulders.**
   You are not being watched.

You are not performing.
You are allowed.

6. **Stay as long as needed.**
   The cloak doesn't expire.
   You can return to it anytime.

Aftercare

Touch your own face gently.
Whisper:
"This version of me is allowed."

RESTORATION RITES

What Are Restoration Rites?

Practices for coming home to yourself, gently, slowly, and without shame

When the world wrings you out
when rage simmers, grief lingers, or numbness settles in
you don't always need to be fixed.
You need to be met.
You need a way back to yourself.

Restoration Rites are not rewards.
They are not aspirational routines or productivity hacks.
They are sacred acts of repair.
Simple ceremonies that restore presence, coherence, and worthiness
to the place you live most: your body.

What Are They For?

Each rite in this section is designed to:
• Offer non-performative comfort
• Rekindle sacred relationship with your body
• Restore your right to take up space again

Some use touch.
Some use breath.
Some ask for nothing but permission.
They can be done alone, in silence, or with someone who loves you.

They don't require readiness.
They don't require words.
They just ask for a moment.

If you're reading this,
you've likely survived something invisible.

You don't have to justify your ache
to reclaim your space in the world.

Begin anywhere.
You are still welcome.

Restoration Rites Quick Reference Guide

Choose what speaks to the sensation, not just the story. Variations are included for low-mobility, sensory, or partnered access.

Rite	Use When…	Page
Self-Anointing (Love)	You feel unloved, forgotten, undesirable, or disconnected from tenderness	**421**
Self- Anointing (Variation)	You want to self-anoint but have limited mobility or range of motion	422
Self-Anointing (Partnered)	You want to receive care and tenderness through sacred touch from another	424
The Pulse Press (Fear)	Fear floods your body and you need rhythmic grounding to return	**426**
Pulse Press (Variation)	You need grounding but prefer to lie down, go silent, or use pressure instead of touch	427
Mirror Hunger (Longing)	You ache for something or someone and need to meet it with grace instead of shame	**429**
Mirror Hunger (Variation)	You're emotionally saturated or low-visual and need a quieter, internal longing ritual	430
Root Lock (Despair)	You feel powerless, hollow, or like your life-force is leaking out	**431**
Root Lock (Variation)	You're trauma-sensitive or mobility-restricted and need a gentler, breath-based version	432
Grief Rocking Chair (Sorrow)	Sorrow moves through and you need to rock, rhythm, or be held	**433**
Grief Rocking (Variation)	Rocking isn't possible, use sound, texture, or breath repetition instead	434
Grief Rocking (Silent/Tactile Variation)	You're nonverbal, overstimulated, or neurodivergent and need a subtle, sensory-based grief rite	436

If none of them call you, just sit on the threshold. That counts too. **You are not lost. You are in the process of returning.**

THE SELF-ANOINTING *(For Love)*

☼ *A ritual to restore warmth, worthiness, and welcome in your own skin.*

Use this when you feel unloved, forgotten, undesirable, or disconnected from tenderness.

You'll Need

- A scented oil, body lotion, or balm (even coconut oil or olive oil is fine)

Do This

1. Place the oil in your palms. Rub to warm.

2. Begin at your feet and anoint upward, slowly applying oil as if to someone sacred.

3. As you touch each area, say aloud: *"You are still worthy of love."*

4. Linger at the heart. Let your hands rest there. Whisper: *"Come home, beloved."*

Aftercare

Wrap yourself in something soft.
Let your scent remind you: *I am allowed to be cared for.*

The Self-Anointing (For Love) (Variation)

☼ *A ritual to restore warmth, worthiness, and welcome in your own skin*

Use this when you feel unloved, forgotten, undesirable, or disconnected from tenderness.

This is not about beauty. This is about belonging. Return to your own skin.

Alternate Access Note

For touch aversion, fatigue, limited mobility, or assistance-based care

You do not need to anoint every part of your body. You do not even need to use oil. **Ritual listens to intention.**

This practice can be done through **symbolic touch**, **partnered care**, or even **mental tracing** if physical movement is not accessible.
Each version is complete.

You'll Need

- A scented oil, body lotion, or balm
  (coconut oil, olive oil, or no oil at all)

Do This

1. **Place the oil in your palms and rub gently to warm.**
   If scent is overwhelming, use an unscented balm or imagine the warmth instead.

2. **Begin at your feet and move upward.**
   Anoint yourself **as if tending to someone sacred.**
   If that's too much today, anoint **only your hands or heart.**
   That is enough.

3. **As you touch each area, say aloud (or think):**
   "You are still worthy of love."

4. **Pause at the heart.**
   Let your hands rest there, or simply hover, or imagine the weight.
   Whisper:
   "Come home, beloved."

Aftercare

Wrap yourself in something soft.
Let your own scent, or even just the memory of care, remind you:
"I am allowed to be cared for."

The Self-Anointing *(Partnered)*

☼ *A ritual for receiving love when your body needs support to remember it*

This version is for those who cannot anoint themselves
whether from illness, injury, fatigue, or sacred need.
It can be offered by a partner, caregiver, nurse, or trusted loved one.

The giver is not saving.
The receiver is not broken.

This is care, not correction.
This is love, not rescue.

Partner Access Notes

- The **giver must be invited** or explicitly permitted.
- The **receiver may stop the ritual at any time**.
- Silence is honored.
- There is no pressure to feel grateful.
- The one being anointed holds the center.

You'll Need

- A gentle oil or balm
- Towels or soft fabric
- A quiet space or moment

Do This

1. **Giver warms the oil in their hands.**
   Rub slowly.
   Let the warmth settle.
   No rush.

2. **Giver places a hand gently on the receiver's chosen starting point,**
   hands, shoulders, or feet.

Ask (or confirm in advance):
"Is this okay?"
Only continue with clear, calm yes.

3. **Begin the anointing.**
   Move slowly. Speak softly.
   At each part, say aloud to the receiver:
   "You are still worthy of love."

4. **When you reach the heart (or stop point), pause.**
   Both partners breathe.
   The giver says:
   "Come home, beloved."

5. **The receiver may respond, or say nothing.**
   Let stillness be enough.
   Let rest be the closing rite.

Aftercare

Cover the receiver with a blanket, towel, or favorite clothing.
Let them rest.
The giver may say:
**"You are loved.
You do not have to earn it."**

Then leave space.
Silence is part of the spell.

THE PULSE PRESS *(For Fear)*

☼ *A ritual to calm fear by pressing back into the rhythm of your own aliveness.*

Use This When

You feel scared, braced, or shaky, especially when fear shows up as racing thoughts or frozen limbs.

You'll Need

- Just your hands.
- Optional: a heavy object like a book or pillow.

Do This

1. **Place your fingers or flat palm directly on your pulse, wrist, neck, or heart.**

2. **Breathe with it.** Count your pulse silently. Let yourself feel: *I am still here.*

3. **Apply gentle pressure with your hand, or rest a comforting weight (like a book) on your chest or belly.**

4. **Repeat this phrase (3x, outloud, if possible):** *"Fear, you don't have to run the whole show."*

Aftercare

Stand barefoot if you can.
Feel the ground.
Say: *My body remembers safety.*

The Pulse Press (For Fear) (Variation)
☼ *A ritual to calm fear by pressing back into the rhythm of your own aliveness*

Use this when you feel scared, braced, or shaky, especially when fear arrives as racing thoughts, frozen limbs, or disconnection. This is not a ritual of control. It's a ritual of return.

Alternate Access Notes

For low sensation, speech limitations, or non-standing bodies

You do not need to feel your pulse, speak aloud, or stand for this to work.
This ritual can be done entirely through **intention, breath, or symbolic pressure. Fear will recognize the signal.**

You'll Need

- Your hands
- Optional: a comforting object like a pillow, book, or weighted wrap

Do This

1. **Place your fingers or palm on your pulse point.**
   Use wrist, neck, or over the heart, wherever sensation is accessible.
   If you cannot feel a pulse, place your hand anyway. The body remembers.

2. **Breathe gently.**
   Count your breath or imagine the beat.
   Say silently:
   "I am still here."

3. **Apply gentle pressure with your hand,**
   or rest a comforting object across your chest or belly.
   If touch is not accessible,
   imagine the weight pressing you gently back into the moment.

4. **Repeat this phrase three times, aloud or internally:**
   "Fear, you don't have to run the whole show."

If speech isn't available,
think it, tap it, or blink once per word.
Ritual listens to intent.

Aftercare

If standing feels safe, stand barefoot and feel the ground.
If not, place your hand on something solid: your bedframe, the wall, your own leg.

Say (or think):
"My body remembers safety."

THE MIRROR HUNGER (for Longing)

☼ *A ritual to honor longing without shame by meeting your own gaze with tenderness and truth.*

When you ache for something
you cannot name,
when it coils behind the ribs
or leaks out as tears
the hunger is not shameful.
Witness it.

You'll Need

- A mirror (any size)
- A quiet moment
- Your face

Do This

1. **Sit or stand in front of the mirror.** Meet your own eyes. Do not look away.

2. **Say aloud:**

   1. *"I know you."*
   2. *"I see what you ache for."*
   3. *"I will not abandon you in this hunger."*

3. **Gaze softly at your face.** Let it blur. Let it sharpen. Let it shift.

4. **Place your hand on the mirror, or on your chest.** Stay until you feel a shift.

Aftercare

Rinse your hands or face in cool water.
Say: *"The ache is seen. I am still here."*

The Mirror Hunger (For Longing) (Variation)

☼ *For those avoiding visual reflection, navigating low vision, or seeking non-visual self-recognition*

This version of the ritual honors the full sensory spectrum.
Whether you are avoiding mirrors for emotional reasons, living with blindness or low vision, or choosing to work without sight, this sequence meets you where you are, with full dignity and power.

Hunger can be witnessed
without sight.
There are other ways
to reflect.

You'll Need

- A recording device (your phone)
- A quiet space
- Your voice

Do This

1. **Record yourself saying:**
   - "I know you."
   - "I see what you ache for."
   - "I will not abandon you in this hunger."

2. **Play it back.** Let your voice return to you.

3. **Place your hand on your chest or belly.**

4. **Breathe.** Let your own voice bear witness.

Aftercare

Wrap yourself in something soft.
Whisper: "The ache is allowed."

THE ROOT LOCK (for Despair)

☼ *A ritual to reclaim life force by locking into the deep root of your body and remembering you are still here.*

When despair floods the body
when you feel like you're falling through yourself
this is how to anchor the bottom.

You'll Need

- A quiet space (floor, mat, or bed)
- Your body weight
- A towel or cushion (optional)

Do This

1. **Lay on your back** with knees bent, feet flat. Let your hands rest gently on your lower belly.

2. **Engage your pelvic floor**, like a soft internal lift, as though you're stopping a stream of urine. Hold gently for 4 seconds, then release. Repeat 3–5 times.

3. **Press your feet into the ground.** Feel your tailbone root downward. Whisper: *"I am not going anywhere. I am still here."*

4. **Let your breath drop low into the belly.** Expand into your hands. Let the weight of your body remind you: gravity has not forgotten you. You are held.

Aftercare

Drink something warm.
Wrap yourself in fabric.
Stay low for a while.

The Root Lock (For Despair) (Variation)
For seated practice, chronic pain, or limited mobility

This version honors those who move differently. Whether seated by choice, pain, injury, or long-term condition, this adaptation invites grounding and pelvic activation without strain. You are not missing anything. The root still knows how to hold you.

You'll Need

- A chair with back support
- A blanket or heavy scarf
- Your breath

Do This

1. **Sit upright with your back supported.** Let your feet press into the floor.

2. **Place the blanket across your lap** or shoulders like a weighted cloak.

3. **Engage your root** by squeezing your pelvic floor gently, just enough to feel a low hum of effort. Hold for 4 seconds. Release. Repeat 3–5 times.

4. **Breathe into your hands, placed low on your belly.**

5. **Say aloud (or inside):** *"I am not drifting. I am anchored."*

Aftercare

Run your hands over your thighs.
Touch something real.
Stay seated until your breath deepens.

THE GRIEF ROCKING CHAIR (for Sorrow)

☼ A ritual to let sorrow move through you by rocking the body into rhythmic release, one sway at a time.

When sorrow swells
and the body wants motion
but cannot find comfort
rock it.
Let the motion say what words cannot.

You'll Need

- A stable chair that allows rocking, swaying, or rhythmic movement
- A blanket or shawl (optional)
- A quiet corner

Do This

1. **Sit down and wrap the blanket around your shoulders if using.**

2. **Begin a gentle rocking motion**. Side to side or forward and back. Let it be small.

3. **Close your eyes.** Let the rhythm become the voice.

4. **If tears come, let them.** If silence comes, let that too.

5. **Rock until something softens.**

Aftercare

Still yourself. Place both feet flat.
Say: *"The sorrow moved through. I am still here."*

The Grief Rocking Chair (For Sorrow) (Variation 1)

☼ *For wheelchair users, bedrest, motion sensitivity, or sensory overwhelm*

Sorrow needs rhythm,
not mobility.
Repetition is its language.

Let the rocking come from inside.

You'll Need

- A rhythmic sound or texture, like humming, tapping, or fabric to touch
- A resting position that feels safe (wheelchair, bed, reclined)
- A space that allows softness

Do This:

1. **Begin a gentle, repetitive rhythm.**
   You can hum, vocalize low, tap a pattern, or rub your fingers along fabric.
   Let it be barely perceptible if needed.

2. **Choose one phrase to repeat with the rhythm:**
   • **"The sorrow is allowed."**
   • **"This ache has room."**
   • **"I will not rush the grief."**
   Say it aloud, whisper it, or think it silently.

3. **Let the rhythm do the rocking.**
   Breathe with it, however your body allows.
   There is no right pace.
   Let your system choose.

4. **If tears come, let them.**
   If nothing comes, stay anyway.
   Grief has its own tempo.
   Trust the shift.

Aftercare

Rest. Hydrate.
Place a hand on your chest or cheek.
Whisper:
"Even now, I remain."

The Grief Rocking Sequence (Silent/Tactile Variation)

For Deaf/HoH, non-verbal grievers, or those with sound sensitivity

Grief still rocks, even in silence. It still sways, even when the body stays still. This version holds space for those who cannot speak, do not hear, or need quiet to survive.

You'll Need

- A texture to trace (e.g., blanket seam, string, edge of fabric)
- A steady position (bed, chair, supported floor rest)
- Optional: a timer or vibration cue if helpful

Do This

1. **Begin a rhythmic motion.**
   Use your fingers to trace the same path, back and forth, loop and return.
   Let it be subtle. Even imagined.

2. **Choose a silent internal phrase to pulse with the motion.**
   You don't need to say it.
   Just match a thought to each pass:
   - "Allowed."
   - "Staying."
   - "Still here."

3. **Continue tracing for as long as needed.**
   Let the rhythm do the rocking.
   You are still moving,
   even without sound or speed.

4. **If tears come, let them.**
   If stillness remains, that is grief too.

Aftercare

Touch a corner of fabric, a wall, or your own hand.
Think, no need to speak:
"I remain.
And the ache is allowed."

BREAK GLASS
PROTOCOLS

What Are Break Glass Protocols?

Glass Protocols are emergency rites for when everything falls apart

These are not rituals for your best self.
They're for the moment before.

When your throat locks.
When the room tilts.
When shame floods your bloodstream or your hands forget how to move.

Break Glass Protocols are short-form nervous system interventions disguised as acts of survival:

- A breath.
- A towel.
- A sentence.
- A bowl of water.
- A truth whispered in a bathroom stall.

They do not aim to fix.
They are not meditations.
They are engineered for one thing: **Reachability.**

What Are They For?
Each Break Glass Protocol is designed to:

- Interrupt a dysregulation spiral
- Create a real-time bridge back to your body
- Offer dignity and direction in moments of overload

They can be done mid-shutdown, mid-panic, mid-descent.
No preparation. No tools. No grace required.
You don't even need to name what's happening.
You just need to **break the glass** and begin.

Break Glass Quick Reference Guide

Quick-match to your moment. Variations include alternate positions, sensory options, and low-mobility versions.

Protocol	Use When...	Page
BREAK GLASS 1: **Overwhelm Protocol**	When your system is overloaded, chaotic, or spinning	**442**
Alternate Overwhelm Protocol	A dark + breath-based version that works anywhere	444
BREAK GLASS 2: **Numbness Protocol**	When you feel frozen, checked-out, or like you're not here	**446**
Alternate Numbness Protocol	Uses scent + sound to gently reawaken presence	448
BREAK GLASS 3: **Rage Protocol**	When heat builds and you fear you'll explode or implode	**450**
Alternate: Rage (No Voice / Public-Safe)	Uses compression + low-sound release for discreet spaces	452
BREAK GLASS 4: **Collapse Protocol**	When your body says "I can't" and everything shuts down	**454**
Alternate: Collapse (Chair / Low Touch)	Weighted grounding + soft presence for seated or low-touch care	456
BREAK GLASS 5: **Grief Spiral Protocol**	When sorrow surges or tears feel endless	**458**
Alternate Grief Protocol	Rocking, warmth, and touch-based witness	460
BREAK GLASS 6: **Panic Protocol**	When your heart races and reality feels warped	**462**
Alternate: Panic (Low-Light / No Speech)	Object tracking + tactile reset without speaking	464
BREAK GLASS 7: **Longing Protocol**	When you ache for something missing or unnamed	**466**

Alternate: Longing (Text-Based / Nonverbal)	Paper rituals + phone-based tethering when words won't come	468
BREAK GLASS 8: **Shame Protocol**	When blame floods you or you feel fundamentally unworthy	**470**
Alternate: Shame (Limited Mobility/ Nonverbal)	Imagination-based grounding, no movement required	472
BREAK GLASS 9: **I Don't Know What I'm Feeling Protocol**	When your feelings are fogged, flat, or impossible to name	**473**
Alternate: IDK Protocol (Voice Memo / Visual)	Uses voice notes + visual tools for unclear states	475

You do not have to be wise, healed, or strong to use these.

You don't even have to be okay.

You just have to be here.

Even if "here" is the floor.
Even if "here" is the stall.
Even if "here" is one shaky breath.

Break the glass.
And start with what you *can* reach.

And begin.

BREAK GLASS 1: OVERWHELM PROTOCOL
A nervous system reset for sensory and emotional overload

Use this when your system goes into shutdown, panic, dissociation, or white-noise spirals.

This ritual reboots the body through **containment, rhythm, and darkness**, without urgency.

You'll Need

- Just your breath + your body
- Optional: towel or blanket

Do This

1. **Find a wall.**
   Press your back, shoulder blades, and heels into it.
   Let it hold you.
   Say (aloud or in your mind):
   "I'm allowed to be held."

2. **Inhale through your nose for 4 counts.**
   Exhale through your mouth for 6.
   Repeat this rhythm 3 times.
   Let the wall carry your weight.

3. **Wrap yourself in a towel or blanket like a cocoon.**
   Tuck the ends if needed.
   Whisper:
   "Nothing has to happen right now."

4. **Cover your eyes with your palm or forearm.**
   Let the darkness come.
   If it feels safe, stay until you feel a shift, small or large.
   Even one softened breath is enough.

Aftercare

Run cold water over your wrists if available.
Say aloud: **"I'm not late. I'm right on time."**

Still not okay? Go to page 486 for emergency intervention resources.

Alternate Overwhelm Protocol

When you can't stand, press, or wrap, **containment can still happen.** This version uses **stillness, weight, and internal rhythm** to restore nervous system coherence.

You'll Need

- Your breath
- A towel, heavy object, or visual focus point (optional)

Do This

1. **Sit, recline, or lie down.**
   Let your back rest against something steady like a chair, bed, pillow, or floor.
   Imagine a wall holding you from behind, even if there isn't one.
   Say (internally or aloud):
   "I don't have to hold myself up right now."

2. **Breathe gently.**
   - Inhale for 4 counts
   - Exhale for 6 counts
   Repeat 3 times, *or just count if breath is difficult.*

3. **Place a towel, book, or weighted object across your chest, belly, or thighs.**
   Let the weight signal safety.
   Say:
   "Nothing has to happen right now."

4. **If safe, close your eyes or soften your gaze.**
   If darkness is dysregulating, focus on one object or texture nearby.
   You are still contained.

Aftercare

Touch something cool like water, metal, fabric, or an edge.
If movement isn't available, imagine coolness flowing through your wrists.
Think or whisper:
"I'm not late.
I'm right on time."

Still not okay? Go to page 486 for emergency intervention resources.

BREAK GLASS 2: NUMBNESS PROTOCOL
A ritual for freeze states, disconnection, or emotional flatlining

Use this when your body goes blank.
When you can't feel a damn thing, or when you feel like you've left.
This ritual **brings the signal back online.**
No pressure to feel everything.
Just begin.

You'll Need

- A bowl of cold water (or cup with ice if available)
- Optional: strong scent (orange peel, spice jar, essential oil cap)

Do This

1. **Fill a bowl (or cup) with cold water.**
   Submerge your hands.
   Stay with the sensation.
   Say (aloud or in your mind):
   "I'm still here."
   Name 3 things you feel (wet, cold, sharp, numbing, tingling).

2. **Touch your skin slowly.**
   Start with your arms, neck, or thighs.
   Use gentle pressure, deliberate, not rushed.
   Say:
   **"This is my body.
   I live here."**

3. **Inhale something sharp.**
   Smell a spice jar, citrus peel, peppermint oil, or even your own skin.
   Let the scent break through.

4. **Sit or stand against something solid.**
   Press your spine or palms into a wall, chair, or floor.
   Say:
   **"I am not gone.
   I'm arriving."**

Aftercare

Drink water (not the bowl water).
Blink slowly.
Touch something textured (fabric, stone, hair, wood).
Whisper:
"I'm back."

Still not okay? Go to page 486 for emergency intervention resources.

Alternate Numbness Protocol

When you cannot reach water, tolerate touch, or access scent, you can still signal return. This version uses *intention, vibration, and rhythm* to bring you back gently.

You'll Need

- Your breath
- A stable surface or object near you
- Optional: audio cue or internal mantra

Do This

1. **Place your attention on one part of your body.**
   Your breath.
   Your foot.
   Your throat.
   Anywhere you can *sense* or *imagine* a location.

2. **Tap or press that spot gently, physically or in your mind.**
   • If using a finger, tap 5 times slowly.
   • If not, imagine a tapping.
   Say:
   "I'm still in here."

3. If scent is unavailable or triggering, focus on **temperature** or **texture.**
   Find something smooth, rough, soft, or cool nearby.
   Rest your fingers there, even if only briefly.

4. **Lean into any solid surface.**
   Back of a chair. Headboard. Bedframe.
   Say:
   **"I am not gone.
   I'm arriving."**

Aftercare

If possible, sip water. If not, imagine cool water entering your mouth.
Blink or close your eyes once. Place your hand (or attention) on your chest.
Think or whisper: **"I'm back."**

Still not okay? Go to page 486 for emergency intervention resources.

•

BREAK GLASS 3: RAGE PROTOCOL

A ritual for when the body holds too much heat, pressure, or fury

Use this when you're vibrating with unspoken anger.
When you're clenching your jaw.
When there's a scream backed up in your spine.
This is your release.

You'll Need

- A towel or soft cloth
- A private space (even a bathroom)
- Your breath + voice

Do This

1. **Wrap the towel between both hands.**
   Twist it.
   Grip it like you mean it.
   Let your forearms shake.
   You are not too much. You are not wrong.

2. **Stomp your feet three times, hard.**
   Feel the floor.
   Say aloud:
   "I am HERE.
   My rage is HERE."
   Repeat if needed.

3. **Exhale with sound.**
   Open your mouth.
   Let it rip—a growl, a moan, a roar.
   Keep it safe, but don't silence it.
   Do it **three times.**
   Let your voice carry the charge.

4. **Throw the towel down.**
   Don't fold it. Don't fix it. Just **drop it.**
   Then place one hand on your chest, one on your belly.

Breathe:
    Inhale for 4
    Exhale for 6
Repeat 3 times.

Aftercare

Run cold water over your hands.
Say:
**"That was allowed.
And I'm still mine."**

Still not okay? Go to page 486 for emergency intervention resources.

Alternate Rage Protocol

For mobility limits, silent environments, or non-verbal bodies

This version is for when you cannot grip, stomp, make noise,
when you're in a wheelchair, in public housing, in a hospital bed, or simply cannot
move without harm.

Your rage still gets to come out.
This version uses **pulse, pressure, and thought-to-body transmission.**

You'll Need

- A firm object you can touch or lean on
- A towel, blanket, or edge of clothing
- Your breath or inner rhythm

Do This

1. **Press both hands against each other (flat palms, fists, or imagined pressure).**
   If that's not possible, press your foot to the floor, or your back into the chair or bed.
   Push for 5 seconds.
   Let your body feel the **force.**

2. **Tap or pulse one body part (hand, thigh, toe) three times.**
   If movement isn't possible, do it in your mind.
   As you tap or think the rhythm, say:
   "I am HERE.
   My rage is HERE."

3. **Exhale forcefully—through your nose or lips.**
   If sound is allowed, **hiss**, **grunt**, or **growl**.
   If not, just let your belly push the breath out sharply.
   Repeat 3 times.

4. **Drop the towel or blanket, or picture it being thrown.**
   No folding. No tidying.
   Then place one hand on your chest (or imagine the touch), one on your belly.

452

Breathe:
   In for 4
   Out for 6
Repeat 3x.

Aftercare

Touch a cool surface.
Say (or think):
**"That was allowed.
And I'm still mine."**

Still not okay? Go to page 486 for emergency intervention resources.

BREAK GLASS 4: COLLAPSE PROTOCOL
A ritual for when the body says "I can't" and everything feels hollow

This is not a fix.
This is not an override.

This is a **consensual surrender**
to stillness
to gravity
to stop.

You'll Need

- A heavy blanket, coat, or towel
- A quiet place (bed, couch, floor)
- Just your body

Do This

1. **Lie down or curl inward, whichever feels truest.**
   Let gravity win.
   Let your spine round.
   No posture. No holding.
   Just **drop**.

2. **Drape the blanket over your body like weight.**
   Let it press into you.
   Let yourself be held by something that will not ask you to do more.

3. **Breathe into your belly.**
   Say softly (or think):
   "I don't have to earn my right to pause."
   Repeat until you feel even a flicker of permission.
   A flicker is enough.

4. **Place one palm on your chest.**
   Name one thing that still exists outside the fog.
   It can be:
   - A sound

- A tree
- Your breath
- A crumb of truth

Aftercare

Drink something warm.
Touch something real.
Say:
**"I can stop.
I can stay.
I'm still allowed to be."**

Still not okay? Go to page 486 for emergency intervention resources.

Alternate Collapse Protocol

For seated bodies, public environments, or chronic shut-down states

Not everyone can lie down.
Not everyone has privacy to fall apart.
This version allows **internal collapse**, quietly, invisibly, completely.

You'll Need

- A coat, scarf, or heavy wrap (optional)
- A seated or reclined position
- A place you can stay for at least 90 seconds

Do This

1. **Let your body round.**
   Slouch.
   Drop your shoulders.
   Let your neck release.
   Even in a chair, even on a bus, even at work.
   Just *let go of upright.*

2. **Drape something heavy over your shoulders or lap, if safe.**
   If not, just **imagine** weight sinking into you.

3. **Inhale into your low belly.**
   Exhale longer than you inhale.
   Say internally:
   "I don't have to earn my right to pause."
   Even if you live in this state daily.
   Even then. Especially then.

4. **Touch one small part of yourself (your collarbone, knuckle, elbow).**
   Name one thing still here.
   Something small.
   Something true.

Aftercare

Sip something warm or neutral.
Touch a texture you trust.
Think or whisper:
**"I can stop.
I can stay.
I'm still allowed to be."**

Still not okay? Go to page 486 for emergency intervention resources.

BREAK GLASS 5: GRIEF SPIRAL PROTOCOL

A ritual for when the ache floods in and you feel like you might drown

This isn't to stop the grief.
It's to give it a channel
so it doesn't tear through you
unchecked
and alone.

You'll Need

- A quiet space
- Optional: pillow, blanket, tissue
- Just your breath + body

Do This

1. **Assume a self-holding position.**
   Fetal position.
   Knees to chest.
   Child's pose.
   Let your body curl inward (rounded, protective, sacred).
   You do not have to be upright to be whole.

2. **Breathe slow and low.**
   Place one hand on your belly, one on your chest.
   Say (aloud or silently):
   **"It's okay to feel this.
   I don't have to outrun it."**

3. **Let the tears come. Or not.**
   Rock gently if it helps.
   Moan if it moves.
   Stay still if that's all you have.
   There's no correct grief.
   Just descent.

4. **Name the shape of the grief.**
   Is it a color?

A temperature?
A sound?
Whisper it into your skin.
Give it texture.

Aftercare

Wash your face. Drink water.
Touch something soft.
Whisper:
**"It came.
It moved.
I'm still here."**

Still not okay? Go to page 486 for emergency intervention resources.

Alternate Grief Spiral Protocol

For seated, reclined, frozen, or invisible grief states

Not every body can curl.
Not every grief looks like sobbing.
This version meets you where movement is small and grief lives quietly.

You'll Need:

- A stable place to rest (chair, bed, recline)
- Optional: soft object (pillow, fabric, hair, sleeve)
- Your breath, even if shallow

Do This

1. **Let your body soften or slump, whatever your position allows.**
   You don't need to curl.
   Just let your chest hollow slightly, your jaw slacken.
   If you're upright, lean back and turn slightly inward.
   Let gravity know it's allowed.

2. **Breathe gently. No forced depth. Just rhythm.**
   Place a hand (or your awareness) on your belly.
   Then your chest.
   Say or think:
   **"It's okay to feel this.
   I don't have to outrun it."**

3. **Let yourself feel: quietly, subtly, or vividly.**
   If tears don't come, name the numbness.
   If sound isn't safe, pulse your fingers.
   If nothing moves, just stay.
   Descent can be invisible and still holy.

4. **Give your grief a shape.**
   In your mind or aloud, answer:
      • What does this grief feel like?
      • Is it rough, round, gray, static, aching?
      • What *form* does it want to take?

Say it. Or imagine saying it.
That is enough.

Aftercare

Wipe your eyes, or your memory of crying.
Drink water if available.
Hold something with texture.
Whisper or think:
"It came.
It moved.
I'm still here."

Still not okay? Go to page 486 for emergency intervention resources.

BREAK GLASS 6: PANIC PROTOCOL
A ritual to regulate racing thoughts, tunnel vision, and spiraling dread

Use this when your mind spins,
your chest tightens,
or the world starts to tilt.
This brings you back to **now.**

You'll Need

- Just your breath, your body, and something real to touch
- Optional: cold object (stone, spoon, ice cube)

Do This

1. **Track with your eyes**
   Pick one object in the room
   Move your eyes slowly from left to right, then back again—3 to 5 times.
   Say aloud (or in your mind):
   **"I'm here.
   This is now."**

2. **Do the 5–4–3–2–1 grounding sequence:**
   • 5 things you can **see**
   • 4 things you can **touch**
   • 3 things you can **hear**
   • 2 things you can **smell**
   • 1 thing you can **taste**

3. Name each out loud if possible
   If not, **think them slowly, one by one**

4. **Anchor with your hands**
   Place your palms on something steady (floor, wall, chair, table)
   Push down
   Feel resistance
   Say:
   **"This is real.
   I'm connected."**

5. **Breathe into your belly**
   Inhale for 4 counts
   Exhale for 6 counts
   Repeat 3–5 times
   Let your exhale **lengthen you**

Aftercare

Hold a steady object
Drink something warm or cool
Say:
**"The storm passed.
I stayed."**

Still not okay? Go to page 486 for emergency intervention resources.

Alternate Panic Protocol

For sensory limitations, speech loss, or immobility during panic

Panic doesn't always come loud.
Sometimes it comes silent.
Frozen. Numb. Blurred.
This version is for **when you can't name the things** or reach them.

You'll Need

- A single object to hold, press, or imagine
- A resting position that allows partial focus
- Your breath (or awareness of its rhythm)

Do This

1. **Choose one object to fix your eyes or attention on.**
   This could be visual, tactile, imagined, or even internal (heartbeat, breath).
   Say or think:
   "This is now."

2. **Ground without naming.**
   Skip the list.
   Instead:
   - Tap one finger 5 times

   - Press your foot down 4 times

   - Blink 3 times

   - Hum or exhale twice

   - Think: **"I exist."**

   No need to describe what you see, hear, or feel.
   Presence is enough.

3. **Anchor with whatever you can touch or imagine touching.**
   A blanket. Your thigh. The back of your hand.

If touch isn't possible, imagine something stable beneath you.
Say (or think):
**"This is real.
I'm connected."**

4. **Breathe without measurement.**
   Just notice the exhale.
   Let it soften your shoulders.
   Let it lengthen your body, even if you're still.

Aftercare

Hold something textured or familiar.
If possible, sip water.
Whisper, think, or blink once per word:
**"The storm passed.
I stayed."**

Still not okay? Go to page 486 for emergency intervention resources.

BREAK GLASS 7: LONGING PROTOCOL
A ritual for the ache that wants something you can't name

Use this when the pull returns
not sadness
not panic
but that ache that wraps around the ribs
and whispers:
"There has to be more."

You'll Need

- Paper + pen (or digital tool)
- Optional: fire-safe place to burn
- A quiet corner. Just you.

Do This

1. **Name the ache.**
   Say aloud (or think):
   "Something in me is reaching."
   Pause.
   Let your body answer.
   Where does the yearning live?
   - Chest
   - Throat
   - Gut
   - Behind the eyes
   Place a hand there if you can.

2. **Write a letter to what you miss.**
   It doesn't need a name.
   Begin with:
   "To the thing I've been waiting for…"
   Let it spill.
   Desire, confusion, grief, memory, hunger.
   Don't edit.

3. **Release it.**
   Burn it.
   Tear it.
   Fold and place it in a jar.
   Delete it.
   Shut the notebook.
   Walk away.
   Say:
   **"I release what I cannot hold.
   I make space for what's real."**

4. **Hold yourself through the ache.**
   Sit or lie down.
   Wrap arms around shoulders or hold a pillow.
   Breathe into the wanting.
   Let it ache.
   No fixing. Just witness.

Aftercare

Touch your heart.
Say:
**"Not everything has a name
but I still matter."**

Still not okay? Go to page 486 for emergency intervention resources.

Alternate Longing Protocol

For blind/low-vision readers, non-writing bodies, public spaces, or chronic yearning states

Not all longing needs paper.
Not all ache can be written down.
This version is for those who hold longing in **the body, not the hands.**
Who return to it **often, not occasionally.**

You'll Need

- A quiet moment
- Your breath
- Optional: voice note, tactile object, or mantra

Do This

1. **Name the ache, without precision.**
   Say or think:
   "Something in me is reaching."
   No need to know what for.
   Just *let the ache have a shape.*

2. **Speak or tap a letter into the air.**
   Say aloud:
   "To the thing I've been waiting for…"
   You can whisper it.
   Think it.
   Tap your fingers in rhythm as if sending Morse code.
   Let it move through you, not through words.

3. **Release the act.**
   Close the screen.
   Set down the device.
   Breathe and say:
   **"I release what I cannot hold.
   I make space for what's real."**

4. If using a tactile object—place it somewhere safe.
   Let it hold the ache for you.

5. **Embrace yourself gently.**
   Lean back.
   Wrap in a blanket.
   Touch your face or chest.
   Don't force comfort.
   Just stay.

Aftercare

Say, or think, slowly:
"Not everything has a name.
But I still matter."
Repeat as needed.

Still not okay? Go to page 486 for emergency intervention resources.

BREAK GLASS 8: SHAME PROTOCOL
When your system floods with shame, use this

This protocol restores clarity when shame hijacks your body, floods your mind, or whispers that you're the problem.

You'll Need

- Just your breath
- A private space (even a bathroom stall)

Do This

1. **Sit or kneel with your spine curved inward.**
   Let your body curl. Round your back.
   This is not collapse, it's protection.

2. **Whisper:**
   "I am not bad.
   Something painful happened."
   Repeat three times, slowly.

3. **Place one hand over your heart, one over your gut.**
   Hold both gently. Breathe. Stay.

4. **Identify one person, animal, or being (even a tree or memory) who would not blame you.**
   Speak their name aloud.
   Let their presence interrupt the spiral.

Aftercare

Wash your hands or splash your face.
Whisper:
"I return without punishment."

Alternate Shame Protocol

For limited mobility, non-verbal users, or those unable to access emotion

This version is for when you can't kneel, curl, or feel anything yet.
It works through **stillness, breath, and substitution.**

You'll Need

- A seated or reclined position
- A private or quiet moment

Do This

1. Let your body soften.
   You can stay upright, reclined, or supported in bed.
   No need to curl if your body can't or doesn't want to.

2. Say internally (or aloud if safe):
   "I am not bad.
   Something painful happened."
   Repeat three times.
   If speech isn't available, **tap three times**, once for each line.

3. Rest one hand (or awareness) on your chest, and the other on your belly.
   If you cannot touch, just *think of the placement.*
   Stay and breathe.

4. Picture someone or something that doesn't blame you.
   A dog. A tree. A grandparent.
   Say their name.
   If that's not possible, imagine a feeling of neutrality.
   That counts.

Aftercare

Use a damp cloth, a facial wipe, or even just close your eyes.
Think: **"I return without punishment."**

Still not okay? Go to page 486 for emergency intervention resources.

BREAK GLASS 9: I DON'T KNOW WHAT I'M FEELING PROTOCOL

For fog, freeze, or when your emotions don't make sense

This is for when your body goes blank,
your brain goes static,
and the question "How are you?" might as well be a gunshot.

You don't need to *know*.
You just need to begin.

You'll Need

- A pen or pencil + a sheet of paper (or a blank notes app)

Do This

1. **At the top of the page, write:**
   "Right now I feel…"

2. **Free-write for 60 seconds.**
   No punctuation. No edits. No overthinking.
   Let it be messy. Let it be wrong. Let it be nonsense.

3. Circle any word or phrase that feels **hot, heavy, strange, or electric.**
   Even one word is enough.

4. **Place your palm over the circled word.**
   Say aloud (or internally):
   "Something in me is feeling this."

That's all.
That's real.

Aftercare

Tear the page.
Recycle it. Burn it.
Or tuck it away.

Then:
Sip something warm.
Touch your chest.
Be done.

Still not okay? Go to page 486 for emergency intervention resources.

Alternate I Don't Know What I'm Feeling Protocol

For those who can't write, read, or speak, but still feel everything

This version is for when writing is not an option
when your hands don't move,
when language won't come,
when fog lives between you and the words.

You'll Need

- Your breath
- One object you can touch or hold (optional)

Do This

1. Say or think:
   "Right now I feel…"
   Let the rest be a silence.
   Let the blankness count.
   Don't finish the sentence.

2. Begin a **sensory stream.**
   Tap your fingers.
   Move your eyes left to right.
   Touch an object.
   Let the movement replace the writing.

3. Choose one **part of your body** that feels something, even if it's just **numb.**
   Place your hand there.
   Or think of touching it.
   Say:
   "Something in me is feeling this."

That's real.
That's enough.

Aftercare

Wash your hands or your memory. Sip water.
Breathe once with your eyes closed. You made it.

Still not okay? Go to page 486 for emergency intervention resources.

THE MYTH OF
SELF RELIANCE

The Myth Of Self-Reliance

**What shame says right before you ask for help…
and why it's lying.**

You were not designed to hold everything alone. Your nervous system was built for connection.

And yet somewhere along the line, many of us were taught to equate self-containment with self-worth. That needing support meant you were broken, behind, dramatic, or weak.

Shame is loud here. It whispers before you reach out. It builds a wall around your suffering and paints it with "strength."

But shame lies. And here's how:

Common Lies Shame Tells Before You Reach Out

The Lie	The Truth
"Other people have it worse."	Pain isn't a competition. If it hurts, it matters.
"I'll sound dramatic."	You're not dramatic. You're dysregulated. That's different.
"I should be over this by now."	Grief doesn't obey timelines. It obeys truth.
"They'll think I'm weak."	Vulnerability is what strength looks like when it's honest.
"It's not a big deal."	If your body is carrying it, your system thinks it *is*.
"I always get through it eventually."	Survival isn't the same as healing.

You don't have to wait until you're sobbing in a bathroom stall to ask for someone to sit with you.

You don't have to be in crisis to say "This is too much to hold alone."

Asking for help isn't a weakness. It's a form of *returning*.

It's your nervous system remembering that care is not a luxury, it's a requirement of being human.

You are not broken for needing support. You are *breaking the spell* that says love and care must be earned through endurance.

And that is no small thing.

Letter 112: To the One Who Ashamed (or Scared) to Ask for Help

I see how hard you've worked
to look like you're okay.
I see the smile you've perfected,
the "I'm just tired" lie,
the way you show up for everyone else
while quietly disappearing from yourself.

I know how loud your mind gets
right before you reach out.
The debate:
Is it bad enough?
Other people have it worse.
I should be able to handle this.
I don't want to bother anyone.
What if they think I'm weak?
What if they agree?

Shame does that.
It builds a throne out of silence.
It tricks you into thinking that
being strong means being solitary.

But listen to me:
You don't have to collapse to be worthy of care.
You don't have to be screaming, sobbing, or suicidal
to say:
This is too much for me to hold alone.

Asking for help
doesn't mean you're failing.
It means you're remembering
that humans were never meant to carry grief in isolation.

It means you are *choosing to live.*
It means something in you still wants to stay.
That is sacred.

You don't have to be articulate.
You don't have to explain it perfectly.
You don't have to be brave.

You just have to say:
"I need someone to sit with me in this."

That is enough.
You are enough.

There is no shame in wanting to feel less alone.
There is no shame in needing someone to witness your pain.
There is no shame in being a person
with a breaking point.

And you don't have to wait
until you reach yours.

There is a door open for you.
There is a number you can call.
There is a life still reaching toward you
through the noise.

Please take it.

-The Sun

You Are Not The Only One

When grief hits, it lies.

It whispers:

> *"You're the only one who feels this."*
> *"Everyone else has life under control."*
> *"You're falling apart over something small."*

That's a lie.

Here's what the numbers actually say:

INVISIBLE GRIEF

- More than **57%** of U.S. adults experienced the death of a close friend, family member, or pet in the past three years *(Eterneva, 2023)*.
- Around **10–20%** of grievers experience *complicated grief*, long-lasting emotional disruption that impacts daily life *(The Recovery Village, 2023)*.
- Among adults over 40, **nearly one-third** report severe grief symptoms after the death of someone close *(National Institutes of Health, 2020)*.

MENTAL HEALTH & SUICIDAL THOUGHTS

- In 2022, **12.8 million** U.S. adults seriously considered suicide, and **1.5 million** made an attempt *(New York Life Foundation, 2022)*.
- LGBTQ youth are **over 40%** more likely to seriously consider suicide than their peers *(Experience Camps, 2023)*.

GRIEF IN THE WORKPLACE

- Most employers offer **3–5 days** of bereavement leave, yet **66%** of grievers still feel the impact one year later *(The Times UK, 2022)*.
- Nearly **1 in 4** employees is actively grieving while on the job *(Eterneva Workplace Grief Report, 2023)*.

…And Yet

- **39%** of UK adults aged 18–35 feel uncomfortable even *talking* about grief *(Happiful Magazine, 2022)*
- **68%** of Americans want more open grief dialogue, but only **18%** feel equipped to start one *(New York Life Foundation, 2022)*

Final Word

Grief is not rare.
It's not abnormal.
It's the cost of having cared in a world that often makes no room for it.

You are not too broken.
You are not too late.
You are not the only one.

Intentionally left blank. Use for notes, if needed.

BEFORE YOU BREAK:
A MAP FOR SURVIVAL

STOP.

BREATHE IN.

PAUSE.

BREATH OUT.

If you are in acute danger, overwhelmed by suicidal thoughts, or unsure if you're safe to be alone…pause here.

Take one breath.

Then another.

Let this page hold you for a moment.
This is not weakness.
This is not failure.
This is what real care looks like
when the pain gets too big for your own hands.

The following pages have a variety of resources.
Find the one that best fits you.

The right one is the one you contact.

Choose the Support Line that Best Fits

988 Suicide & Crisis Lifeline

For anyone in emotional distress, crisis, or needing someone to talk to.
Support that meets you where you are, without judgment or assumptions.
- 📞 Dial **988** (call or text)
- 🌐 988lifeline.org
- Free. Confidential. 24/7. Human.

BlackLine

Peer support for Black, Brown, Indigenous, and Queer people
especially those navigating state violence, grief, or harm from institutions.

- 📞 1-800-604-5841
- 🌐 callblackline.com
- Peer-run. No police involvement.
- Voicemail available outside hours.

Childhelp National Child Abuse Hotline

If you're a young person who is not safe in your home, or you're an adult supporting someone who isn't.

- **Who it's for:** Children, teens, and adults experiencing or reporting abuse
- 📞 Call or text 1-800-4-A-CHILD (1-800-422-4453)
- 🌐 childhelphotline.org

Crisis Text Line

For anyone who needs to talk, especially when it's too hard to say it out loud
Support that fits in your pocket, when you can't pick up the phone.
- 📱 Text **HELLO** to **741741**

- 🌐 crisistextline.org
- Immediate. Private. Available anytime.

International Support

If you're not in the U.S., or calling 988 isn't possible:

- 🌐 Visit opencounseling.com/suicide-hotlines
  A country-by-country directory of suicide hotlines and emotional support services.

NowMattersNow (DBT Tools for Suicidal Thoughts)

If you're having thoughts you can't say out loud, and you want something structured, proven, and calm.

- **Who it's for:** Anyone experiencing suicidal ideation or intense emotional pain
- **What it offers:** DBT skills, videos, breathing tools, real people sharing what helped
- 🌐 nowmattersnow.org

StrongHearts Native Helpline

For Native and Indigenous people impacted by violence, abuse, or crisis
Support that understands sovereignty, silence, and cultural grief.

- 📞 1-844-762-8483
- 🌐 strongheartshelpline.org
- Culturally rooted. Confidential. Trauma-informed.

The Trevor Project

For LGBTQIA+ youth and young adults (ages 13–25)
You can call, chat, or text, even if you don't have the words.

- 📞 1-866-488-7386
- 🌐 thetrevorproject.org/
- 📱 Text START to 678-678 (U.S. only)

Trans Lifeline

For trans and nonbinary people, by trans and nonbinary people
No non-consensual rescue. No gatekeeping. Just someone who *gets it.*

- 📞 U.S.: 877-565-8860
- 📞 Canada: 877-330-6366
- 🌐 translifeline.org
- Peer-run. No police. No forced intervention.

Veterans Crisis Line

If you've served, or are serving, and your pain feels too complex for civilian ears, go here.

- 🌐 veteranscrisisline.net
- Available 24/7, for veterans, service members, and their families.

How To Ask For Help

Because sometimes the hardest part
isn't needing help,
it's saying it out loud.

You don't need to be calm.
You don't need to be fluent.
You don't need to explain it all in the right order.

You just need to begin.

If your voice is shaking...
If your body is numb...
If all you can manage is a whisper or a typed line...
Let it be this:

Sample Scripts

- "I don't feel okay."
- "I'm scared, and I don't know what to do."
- "I don't want to die, but I don't want to feel like this anymore."
- "I need someone to stay with me for a minute."
- "Please don't escalate. I'm not a danger. I just need someone to witness me."
- "I'm experiencing racial trauma. Please don't dismiss it."
- "I don't have the words. Please stay with me."

If You're Not Sure What You Want

That's okay. Try:
- "Can you just listen?"
- "I'm not asking for solutions. I just need presence."
- "Can we breathe together for a minute?"
- "I need to be reminded I'm not alone."

You Can Say This Too:

- "I'm afraid you'll judge me."
- "I'm afraid I'll say something wrong."
- "I'm afraid you won't believe me."

Naming the fear is not a mistake.
It's an act of courage.

What If You Don't Say Anything At All?

That's okay too. You can:

1. Text instead of speak
2. Chat online without turning on your mic
3. Sit in silence while someone holds the line

Someone will still stay with you.

Final Reminder

You do not have to be articulate to be in crisis.
You do not have to be coherent to be cared for.
You do not have to be calm to be taken seriously.

You only have to be here.
You only have to reach.
You only have to want to stay.

JOURNALING
PAGES

Letters that Resonated With Me

Letter _____: _____

_____

_____

_____

_____

_____

_____

_____

_____

_____

_____

Letter _____: _____

_____

_____

_____

_____

_____

_____

_____

_____

_____

_____

Letter _____: _____

_____

_____

_____

_____

_____

_____

_____

_____

_____

_____

Letter _____: _____

_____

_____

_____

_____

_____

_____

_____

_____

Letter _____: _____

_____

_____

_____

_____

_____

_____

_____

_____

Letter _____: _____

_____

_____

_____

_____

_____

_____

_____

_____

This template is available for download at www.invisible-grief.com

My Letter

This letter doesn't need to make sense to anyone but you. If you are stuck, you can take lines from the letters in this book that stuck to you and form your own. When you are done, you can destroy the letter or keep it and come back to it. All that matters is you name it and get it out of your head.

_____

_____

_____

_____

_____

_____

_____

_____

_____

_____

_____

_____

_____

_____

_____

_____

_____

_____

_____

_____

_____

_____

_____

_____

_____

_____

_____

_____

_____

_____

_____

_____

_____

_____

_____

_____

_____

_____

_____

_____

_____

_____

_____

_____

_____

_____

_____

_____

_____

_____

_____

_____

_____

_____

_____

_____

_____

_____

_____

_____

_____

_____

_____

_____

This template is available for download at www.invisible-grief.com

About the Author

(or: The One Who Refused to Leave It Unwritten)

This book wasn't born in a writing retreat or over a glass of wine.
It was born in grief.
Invisible.
Unrelenting.
The kind that guts you slowly while the world keeps going.

I wrote these letters at the edge of my own life. In the in-between.
Between paychecks.
Between breakdowns.
Between knowing who I was and wondering if I'd ever get back to her.

No one came to save me.
So I wrote the thing I wished someone had handed me when everything was falling apart.

This isn't a brand. It's a lifeline.
It's not just a book. It's a field kit.
And if it's in your hands now, maybe you needed it, too.

People ask why the letters are signed by *The Sun.*

Here's why:
Because that's who I had to become to survive.
Because sometimes, the part of you that still believes in light has to write the letter until the rest of you catches up.

—Nikkia (aka The Sun)